The New West End Synagogue Guild

Generations

Over 100 recipes from
a culinary community

Published by Creative Interpartners, London
Email: ci@creativeinterpartners.co.uk

ISBN: 978-0-9566706-0-1

For Sharlott Toube,
who loved to cook

Foreword

I am delighted to write a few words for this very special cookery book
'Generations'. Recipes through the generations, passed on through
families, or rediscovered in well-thumbed cookbooks on the shelf, give
a real feeling of continuity. I am especially excited that this book is the
creation of different generations of the New West End Guild:
women working and creating together.

Well done, ladies and good luck with this lovely book

Lady Elaine Sacks

welcome

Welcome to Generations,
the cook book of the New
West End Synagogue. The
Guild embarked on a project
to produce this book and
raise money for the many
and varied charities that
they support.

welcome!

This is a collection of recipes from all the community, young and old: recipes from children and from grandmothers, from our many friends in London and around the world. We have tried hard to introduce some interesting and different recipes to you. Thank you to everyone who has given us their favourite recipes – we are sorry we did not have room in the book to use them all.

There are many people who have helped make this project possible. We would like to thank all our sponsors, in particular Felicity and Frank Miller and their family, together with our very generous supporters and all our wonderful advertisers. Thanks must go to all the community who have put in messages and greetings. Without them we could not have produced this book and continued the good work of the Guild.

Some very special people have worked very hard in producing and editing the book. Shana Ballon took on the task of retyping and transcribing the recipes. Sheli Rodney has collated, edited, proof-read and got the entire text ready to be sent Caryl Harris's team at Creative Interpartners. Caryl and her team, Kate Melsom, Heloise Ralantoaritsimba, Daisy Argyle and Jo Barratt have used their considerable design skills to present the recipes in an exciting and stylish way. They have given many hours of their time organising the printing and production. They have all been amazing. We were very fortunate in having their expertise at our disposal and we appreciate all their hard work.

A very big 'thank you' must go to Shirley Anderson for her illustrations throughout the book, as well as to Jonathan Kennedy for his fantastic photographs.

Of course special thanks must go to the Guild committee who have supported this project and helped bring it to fruition: Valerie Green, Susan Katz, Natalie Cutler, Debbie Talalay, Renee Richman, Valerie Richman, Patricia Fisher and Gaby Morris. Rabbi Geoffrey Shisler has also helped and encouraged us and he will be very pleased not to have pages of recipes lying around the house!

Finally we thank you for buying our book. Please recommend it to all your friends. We hope you have many happy hours around the dining table enjoying our selection of recipes, knowing that you will have also helped many worthwhile charities.

Anne Shisler

Sovereign Photography

The New West End Synagogue is among the most beautiful and historic buildings of Jewish interest in England and was only the second synagogue in the country to be designated a Grade 1 Listed Building by English Heritage. The Foundation Stone was laid on 7th June 1877 by Mr. Leopold de Rothschild in the presence of the Chief Rabbi, Dr. Nathan Marcus Adler, and the building was formally opened on 30th March 1879. The building bears many similarities to the Princes Road Synagogue in Liverpool, which had been designed by the same architect, George Audsley, shortly before the New West End was planned.

The founder members were the crème de la crème of Victorian Jewry and included such famous families as the Rothschilds, the Samuels, the Montagues and the Spielmans. In the 1930s the membership included Lord Rothschild, who had received the Balfour Declaration as a representative of the Jewish people, Sir Herbert (later Lord) Samuel, the first British High Commissioner in Palestine, and Dr Chaim Weizmann, later the first President of the State of Israel.

The first Minister was Rev Simeon Singer (of Singer's Prayer Book fame) from 1879 until his death in 1906. Amongst his successors was Rev Ephraim Levine (Minister from 1916 - 1954 and subsequently Emeritus Minister) and recipes from his sisters Leah and Rachel are included in this book.

The New West End is the most popular setting for United Synagogue weddings, combining unparalleled ambience with a convenient location for Central London reception venues.

The Synagogue's treasures include some twenty Sifrei Torah, as well as superb examples of embroidery and silver, some dating back to the early eighteenth century. Visitors are welcome on Mondays to Thursdays between 10am and 1pm; groups should contact the Synagogue office in advance on 020 7229 2631.

www.newwestend.org.uk

Cooking tips

Quick Key: To make finding the right meal easy, for every recipe you'll see some icons by the title. These indicate at a glance whether this is dairy, meat or parev. Some chefs have made a suggestion as to typical number of servings. This is indicated next to the other icons.

Meat   Dairy   Parev   Serves

Oven temperature conversion guide:

Celsius	Fahrenheit	Gas mark
110	225	1/4 very cool or very slow
130	250	1/2
140	275	1 cool or slow
150	300	2
170	325	3 very moderate
180	350	4 moderate
190	375	5 moderately hot
200	400	6
220	425	7 hot
230	450	8 very hot
240	475	9

Weights & measures: **Metric measures:** the following table is not an exact conversion but a recommended working equivalent.

Grams (g)	Imperial pounds and ounces (lb and oz)
25g	1 oz
50g	2 oz
100g	4 oz
225g	8 oz
350g	12 oz
450g	1 lb
1000g (1kg)	2.2 lb

American and Imperial Measures:

American	Imperial	Cups
16 fluid oz	20 fluid oz	1 pint
8 fluid oz	10 fluid oz	1 cup

Liquid Measures:

Millilitres (ml)	Imperial
150 ml	5 fluid oz (1/4 pint)
300 ml	10 fluid oz (1/2 pint)
600 ml	20 fluid oz (1 pint)
1000 ml (1 litre)	1 3/4 pints

Unit Abbreviations:

Tablespoons, teaspoons and equivalents

Most measuring spoons are marked as:

1 tablespoon (tbsp) = 15 ml

1 dessert spoon = 10 ml

1 teaspoon (tsp) = 5 ml

Soups

While chicken soup is a long-standing staple of the traditional Friday night meal, it can be fun to try out different colours and flavours. Here we bring you every shade of the rainbow, and even a double soup made of two complementary colours. Enjoy!

Tomato soup

Sylvia Hartman

Preparation time: 1hour 10mins

1kg soft Tomatoes
2 Carrots
2 medium Onions
Salt and pepper
1 tsp Vinegar
1 tsp Sugar or sweetener
1/2 litre Water

Peel and slice carrots and onions. 'Sweat' the onions in a little oil (not olive) until transparent. Add the carrots and stirring, sweat for a further 15 minutes. It is important not to let them burn.

Wash the tomatoes and cut in half to check they are good inside, add to the saucepan and add salt and pepper to taste, vinegar and sugar or the equivalent in sweetener. Allow to cook down a bit and keep stirring.

Add half a litre of water.

Cook for approximately three quarters of an hour on a simmer light (stir occasionally) until the carrots are soft, this will indicate that everything is cooked enough.

Allow to cool slightly and either blend in the saucepan or in a liquidiser or Magimix. Taste. Adjust seasoning if necessary.

Parsnip soup

Linda Lewin

Preparation time: 1hour 10mins

1 oz Butter or margarine
1 lb Parsnips, peeled and chopped
1 medium Onion
1 tsp Curry powder
1$^{1/2}$ pints Milk or milk substitute
1$^{1/2}$ pints Stock
Salt
Fresh pepper
Chopped parsley for garnish

Melt butter/margarine and add parsnips and onion. Cook for 10 minutes stirring frequently. Add curry powder and cook 2-3 minutes. Add stock, milk, salt and pepper and bring to the boil.

Simmer for 1 hour. Blend or sieve. Adjust seasoning when re-heating.

With best wishes for the success of this recipe book, Martin and Linda Lewin

Jerusalem artichoke soup

Debbie Talalay

Preparation time: 25mins

▌▐▌▐▌▐▌▐▌▐▌▐▌▐▌▐▌▐▌▐▌▐▌▐▌▐

Soup
2 lbs Jerusalem artichokes
1 large Onion
Milk
Butter
Mace

Garnish
Chives
Cream (optional)
2 slices of Brown bread
reduced to breadcrumbs
(optional)

Finely chop the onion and sauté in butter. Peel or scrub the artichokes well, slice thinly and boil in water until tender. (If you have scrubbed the artichokes the water may need to be thrown out.)

Liquidise the onions and artichokes together. Add a little mace. Add milk and/or water until you have a good consistency for soup and cook for a further 10 minutes.

Gently sauté brown breadcrumbs in butter.

Garnish with breadcrumbs and chives and a dollop of cream in each bowl as you serve.

Curried pea and apple soup

Val Margolis

Preparation time: 20mins

1 oz Butter
1 Onion
2 tsp Curry power, mild
2 Granny Smith apples
2 cups Frozen peas
Half lettuce,
shredded (soft lettuce)
3 cups Vegetable stock
1/2 cup Milk (optional)

Chop the onion, peel and chop the apples.

Heat butter in a pot, add onion and curry powder. Cook, stirring for approximately 2 minutes. Add apples, peas, lettuce and stock, then bring to the boil, reduce the heat and simmer for 10 minutes or until the peas are tender. Purée in a processor or blender in batches until smooth. Add milk and reheat before serving.

Tip

Can be frozen in a sealed container for up to two months.

Wishing the Guild every success with their wonderful cookery book, Jeff and Val Margolis

Sweet potato and red pepper soup

Irene Leeman

Preparation time: 40mins

||||||||||||||||||||||||||||||||||||||||

500g Sweet potato
2 medium Red peppers
1 large Onion
3 Garlic cloves
1.2 litres Vegetable stock
1-2 Chillies
300ml Dry white wine
(optional)

Peel and cube the sweet potato, or leave the skins on for a more rustic texture/flavour. Deseed and roughly chop the peppers and chillies. Crush the garlic cloves.

Put all ingredients into a saucepan, bring to the boil and then simmer for 30 minutes. If you are not using the white wine then use more vegetable stock.

Season with freshly ground black pepper.

||||||||||||||||||||||||||||||||||||||||

Tom Yum (Thai spicy soup)

Mandy Shaw

Preparation time: 30mins

||||||||||||||||||||||||||||||||||||||

6 cups Vegetable stock
2 stalks Lemongrass
3 whole Kaffir lime leaves
2 cups Soft tofu
1-2 red Chillies
4 Cloves of garlic
1 thumb-size piece Ginger
1 cup Mushrooms
2 cups Baby pak choi
1 cup Cherry tomatoes
1/2 can good-quality
Coconut milk (essential)
1 tsp brown sugar
3-4 tbsp soy sauce
1 tbsp fresh-squeezed
Lime juice
1/2 cup fresh Basil
1/3 cup fresh Coriander
(Cilantro)

Slice tofu into cubes, separate the pak choi leaves and chop all other vegetables. If using small button mushrooms these can be used whole.

Combine all ingredients in a saucepan, bring to the boil and then simmer.

Chef's note

If you don't have any pak choi, this spicy soup is also delicious with broccoli.

Adam's pumpkin soup

Toni Nagel

Preparation time: 40mins

▌▐▌▐▌▐▌▐▌▐▌▐▌▐▌▐▌▐▌▐▌▐▌▐▌▐▌

3 cups Butternut Pumpkin
1 medium Carrot
1 Courgette
1 White onion, peeled
and quartered
675ml Stock
(chicken, vegetable
or bullion)
Salt and pepper

Peel and cube the pumpkin, carrot and courgette.
Peel and quarter the onion.

Place all ingredients into a pot. If the vegetables are not covered
by the stock, add water to cover. Bring to the boil and simmer at a
moderate heat, partially covered until the carrots are tender, this
should take about 30 minutes.

Blend until smooth and then add salt and pepper to taste.

Garnish can be a basil leaf, sour cream (if the soup is parev) or
simply some toasted crusty bread.

▌▐▌▐▌▐▌▐▌▐▌▐▌▐▌▐▌▐▌▐▌▐▌▐▌▐▌

Egg and lemon soup with meatballs

Felicity Miller

Preparation time: 50mins

▌▐▌▐▌▐▌▐▌▐▌▐▌▐▌▐▌▐▌▐▌▐▌▐▌▐▌▐▌

The Soup
2¼ lbs of Minced beef
1 medium Onion, diced
1 tbsp chopped Fresh parsley
1/2 tsp ground Allspice
1/2 tsp ground Cloves
2 Eggs
1/3 cup of uncooked American long grain rice
1 tsp Sea salt
1/2 tsp ground black Pepper
8 cups of Water
or mix of beef stock and water

For the egg and lemon sauce:
2 Eggs
Juice of 3 Lemons

Make meatballs: combine minced beef, onion, parsley, allspice, cloves, 2 eggs, 1/3 cup of uncooked rice, salt, and pepper. Form the meat into 30-32 small (1¹ᐟ² inch) meatballs. (If you prefer, you can leave the rice out of the meatballs and put it directly into the soup - this is what I generally do.)

Make soup: Bring 8 cups of water/beef stock/mixture to a boil. Add meatballs and rice. When it returns to a full boil, cover and simmer for 30 minutes. (If you want to freeze the soup/keep it for later, do it at this stage. If you want to serve immediately, make the egg and lemon sauce as follows.)

Make egg and lemon sauce: Beat 2 eggs until frothy. Slowly add lemon juice while beating continuously until blended. Add 8 large tablespoonfuls of liquid from the soup to the egg-lemon mixture and whisk to combine. Do not just add egg-lemon mixture to the pot of soup, or you will get scrambled egg soup!

Pour the mixture into the soup and stir well. Remove from heat. Taste for seasoning and add more salt if needed. Cover and let sit for 20 minutes before serving.

▌▐▌▐▌▐▌▐▌▐▌▐▌▐▌▐▌▐▌▐▌▐▌▐▌▐▌▐▌

Pelgritz (barley soup)

Eliane Wasserman

Preparation time: 3hours

1½ lbs Carrots
2 Leeks
4 stems Celery
Half a boiler Chicken
1½ lbs top Rib (beef)
8 oz Butter beans
300g Pearl barley
2 Chicken stock cubes
1 tsp Salt
2-3 pinches Pepper
4 pints Water

Boil water in large saucepan. Wash and cut up all vegetables.

When water boils add chicken and beef first then all the rest of the ingredients with barley last.

Cook on low heat to keep simmering for 2½ to 3 hours. Stir often to avoid sticking.

Check that beef and chicken are tender and top up with water as required. Add any further salt and pepper to taste.

Tip

Leftovers can be re-warmed and served again.

With best wishes from Eliane and Victor Wasserman

Double soup
of carrots and peas

Anna Churnin

Preparation time: 30mins

350g Carrots, peeled
300g Frozen petits pois, defrosted
1 large Onion, peeled & roughly chopped
50g Butter/margarine
2 Chicken/vegetable stock cubes
Salt
Freshly ground black pepper
Water

In a medium sized saucepan, cook the onion in butter/margarine over a low heat for 6-8mins until soft and translucent. Transfer half the onion to another pan. Add 570ml of water to each pan. Add a stock cube to each and bring them to the boil.

Bring another small pan of water to the boil. Take a vegetable peeler and draw it down the length of a few of the larger carrots so that you have 18 ribbons about 10cm long and 1cm wide to use for the garnish. Then blanch these carrots in the small pan of boiling water for 1 minute. Drain, refresh under cold water.

Chop the remaining carrots into 2.5cm chunks. Add the chopped carrots to one of the two pans and the peas to the other. Reduce the heat to a simmer and cook both the peas and carrots for 8-10 minutes until the vegetables are tender. Blend the soups separately until well puréed. Season each soup to taste. Reheat the soups.

Place the carrot ribbons in a piece of foil and heat them through in the oven. To serve, pour the soups into 2 heatproof jugs and simultaneously pour them into warmed soup plates, so that half is carrot and half is pea. Loosely arrange the warmed carrot into curls and garnish each plate with 3 of them. Serve.

Chicken soup

Valerie Green

Preparation time: 3½ hours

1/2 Boiling chicken
(fowl and giblets)
Small fennel
3 or 4 sticks Celery
1 large Onion
2 large Carrots
1/2 a medium Swede
120g approx. Butter beans
1 Chicken soup cube
Salt and pepper
Coriander
Lemon balm

Cut up carrots, swede, fennel and celery. Place chicken in large saucepan and cover with water. Bring to the boil and skim.

Wash butter beans under hot water and add them to the vegetables and all other ingredients into the soup. Bring back to the boil and gently simmer for 3 hours.

Take out the chicken. Take meat off the necks and chop the other giblets. Liquidise vegetables. Return giblet meat to the soup. Add cooked lokshen or kneidlach.

Re-heat when required or freeze in portions.

Note

An alternative twist to your usual Friday night chicken soup!

Nancy's easiest and best matzo balls

Bobby Silver

2 Eggs
1 tablespoon warm Water
2 tsp Powder soup stock
1 tbsp Oil
1/2 cup Matzo meal

Combine all the ingredients.
Let the mixture rest in the fridge for a few hours before making matzo balls.

To cook the matzo balls, boil them in plenty of water.

Chef's note:

This must be the world's best recipe and incredibly easy to make.

Asparagus soup

Valerie Green

Preparation time: 40mins

3 bunches Asparagus
1 Onion soup cube
2 medium Leeks or Onions
1 medium Potato
4 sticks fresh Coriander
1.8 litres Water
Salt and pepper

Prepare the asparagus in the usual way, discarding the woody part of the stem. Chop a small amount of the asparagus, cutting the remainder approximately in half.

Place in a good size saucepan adding all the other ingredients. Cook for 30 minutes. Take out the small chopped pieces and put to one side. Purée and return the chopped pieces into the soup.

Carrot and sweet potato soup

Yvonne Shisler

Preparation time: 45mins

1 large Onion
1 lb Carrots
1 large Sweet potato
1 tbsp parev Vegetable soup mix
Salt and pepper
Coriander

Cut onion, carrots and sweet potato. Place in a large saucepan and fry until slightly transparent, adding salt and pepper.

Add water and soup mix and cook on a low light until very soft. Blend, then add coriander to taste.

Tip

Thicken if required by adding potato.

Gazpacho

Sandra Blackman

Preparation time: 20mins

2 tins Tomatoes
3 oz Breadcrumbs
1 litre Tomato juice
4 tbsp Salad oil
3 tbsp Vinegar
1/2 tsp Garlic salt
3/4 unpeeled Cucumber
1 medium Onion
1 Green pepper
Black pepper

Liquidise the tinned tomatoes and pour into a bowl.

Grate the cucumber and onion and chop the pepper finely.

Add to the tomatoes along with all other ingredients. Chill.

Meat

If you're looking to get away from the same old roast chicken and shake up your Shabbat table, then look no further. And for those who just want to spice up the chicken a little, try some of our delicious additions.

Chicken Hameem

Flora Frank

Preparation time: 25mins
Cook overnight

A Whole roaster chicken
2 Tomatoes, chopped
1 small tin of Tomato purée
2¹ᐟ² - 3¹ᐟ² cups of Basmati rice,
to taste
Chicken pieces to augment
(optional)
Salt and pepper to taste
8-10 pods of Cardamom,
to taste
1 tsp Turmeric
3-6 Cinnamon sticks,
depending on size and taste
dash of Cumin

Wash rice well. (You may wish to soak it in salted water.)
Mix all the above ingredients together, excluding the
chicken. Add water to facilitate 'stuffing'.

Lay the chicken, breast downwards, in a saucepan with a lid.
Stuff the chicken with approximately a third of the mixture.
Sew up or place a giblet or small piece of chicken at the
opening.

Lay the remainder of the rice mixture around the chicken.
Add water to the pot to reach just under the top of the
chicken. Bring to the boil and let the rice almost cook.

Approximately half an hour before Shabbat, place the pot
on a Shabbat hotplate or blech, or in a low oven to cook
overnight. When ready to serve, lift the chicken out with two
large spatulas or spoons and cut in pieces, placing the rice
around the dish. The stuffed rice will be a different texture
to the rice that surrounded the chicken.

Lamb cholent

Jonathan Robinson

Preparation time: 20mins
Cook overnight

2-3 lbs Diced lamb
2 Garlic cloves
3 tablespoons oil
4 Sprigs mint
1/2 cup White wine
5 Potatoes, peeled and quartered
1 cup Kidney beans
2 cups mixed with dried Raisins, dried Apricots and dried Pears
dried Rosemary
2 tbsp Sugar

Rub the lamb with garlic, brown in hot oil.

Put in slow cooker and sprinkle with seasoning. Place mint sprigs over the lamb and add wine. Place potatoes, beans, dried fruit, rosemary and sugar around the lamb.

Fill the pot with water, bring to the boil and simmer until Shabbat lunch – delicious!

Best wishes
from
Jonathan Robinson

Chicken breasts with raspberry vinegar

Diana Vernon, Head Teacher, City of London School for Girls

Pre-heat your oven to 375°F
Preparation time: 25mins
Cooking time: 30mins

8 Chicken breasts
Oil
2 tbsp Pink peppercorns, crushed
1 large Spanish onion, chopped
6 tbsp Raspberry vinegar
4 tsp Redcurrant jelly, to taste
Salt and pepper, to taste

Editor's note

As it is very difficult to find kosher raspberry vinegar, see opposite for our recipe.

Fry chopped onion, in a saucepan, until soft and transparent, but not caramelised. Add raspberry vinegar and redcurrant jelly and stir until hot through. (Vinegar will hit the back of your throat – beware!)

Tenderise chicken breasts, lightly oil and rub peppercorns into the chicken and season lightly with salt (and ordinary pepper if you wish). Place breasts into an oiled baking dish and cover with onion, vinegar and jelly mixture.

Cover the dish with silver foil and place in oven for 25–30 minutes at 375°F, until chicken breasts are cooked through. If you prefer, after rubbing the peppercorns in the chicken, you can sear the chicken quickly in a lightly oiled frying pan prior to baking, in which case you will probably only need 20 minutes in the oven.

Serve with new potatoes, green vegetables or salad and garnish with raspberries!

Raspberry vinegar

Preparation time: 5 days

125g Raspberries
(over-ripe ones are fine)
350ml distilled
or white wine Vinegar

Prepare the raspberries, wash (and inspect) the raspberries under cold running water and drain thoroughly. Use a fork to lightly mash the raspberries. Add the vinegar of your choice and let it mature for 5 days.

At this stage you can either strain the vinegar through a fine sieve into sterilised bottles/jars or it you can bottle it as it is. However if the raspberries are kept, the vinegar may lose its attractive red colour after a while.

Keep refrigerated.

Chef's note

Other soft fruits can be used to make flavoured vinegars of your own choice

Nana's meatballs

Shirley Anderson

Preparation time: 30mins
Cooking time: 1½hours

2 medium Onions
Sunflower oil
1 tbsp Tomato purée
1 tbsp Osem Vegetable soup
and seasoning mix
500g Best beef mince
1 Egg
2 tbsp dried Onions
Medium matzo meal

Dice onions and fry in sunflower oil until softened and slightly golden brown. Drain oil, turn cooked onion into a large, deep-lidded casserole dish and add tomato purée. Add boiling water until a third of the casserole dish is submerged. Add Osem vegetable soup and seasoning mix and stir in until broken down.

In a separate dish turnout the beef mince. Add a fair amount of cold water to soften, egg and pepper. (No salt is needed, as Osem soup mix is already quite salty.) Mix with a fork and break down and soften, if needed add more cold water.

Add dried onions (not pre-fried) to the beef mix. Mix with a fork to soften. Add a little medium matzo meal to bind, remembering that the cold water makes meatballs moist. (Do not drown.) Moisten hands under tap, and roll meatballs, approximately 8-10 medium sized. Then add to the casserole dish and spoon the sauce mixture over meatballs. Put a lid over and cook in medium heat oven for 1$^{1/2}$ hours. Occasionally take out and check with a spoon that bottom of meatballs are not burning. Also occasionally spoon thickened liquid over meatballs.

Orange and cranberry chicken

Joyce King

Pre-heat your oven to 180°C
Preparation time: 15mins
Cooking time: 1½hours

1 Roasting chicken,
divided into 8 portions
2 Oranges
Juice and rind of
1 more orange
1 can Cranberry sauce
2 tbsp Onion soup powder
1/2 glass White Wine

Slice 2 oranges and lay at the bottom of a roasting pan. Lay chicken portions on top. Mix the rind, cranberry sauce and soup powder and spread over the chicken. Pour the orange juice and white wine over the top.

Roast uncovered in medium oven for approximately $1^{1/2}$ hours, or until the chicken is tender.

Buon Appetito,
Renee and
Valerie Richman

Meat loaf

Pamela Hammerschlag

Preparation time: 20mins
Cooking time: 1-1½hours

1kg Mincemeat
2 dessert spoons Matzo meal
1 Onion
1/2 tsp Pepper
1 Telma soup cube
1 Tomato
1 Granny Smith apple, peeled and cored
Extra Onion and tomato for topping
Oil
Gravy

Put matzo meal, onion, pepper, soup cube, tomato and apple into the food processor and chop well. Add the mince to chopped ingredients by hand and mix well.

Shape into a loaf and put into large roasting pan. Cover with sliced onions and tomato. Pour over 2-3 tablespoons of oil and bake for 1–1½ hours.

Menu tip

Surround the loaf with potatoes and add a bisto gravy 20 minutes before the end of the cooking time.

Liver with green beans

Lynn Brown

Preparation time: 10mins
Cooking time: 50mins

1 lb Ox liver cut into
1-inch strips
1 tbsp Plain flour
Salt and pepper
1 Onion, diced
1 tbsp Oil or Margarine
1 pt beef stock (or other liquid)
1-2 tbsp vegetarian*
Worcestershire sauce
1 tbsp Wine or Cider Vinegar
Salt and pepper
1 lb sliced Green Beans
(can be frozen)
Cornstarch for thickening

Place liver pieces into plastic bag with 1 tablespoon of flour and salt and pepper. Shake to coat.

Soften onion in oil or margarine in large saucepan. Add the liver to brown over. Add the pint of beef stock or enough fluids to cover the meat, together with Worcestershire sauce and wine or cider vinegar, salt and pepper. Stir quickly to get a smooth coating of sauce and cook for 30-45 minutes until the liver is tender.

Add green beans (can still be frozen) and stir, cook until softened. Stir 1 tablespoon of cornflour into a little cold water and add to meat to thicken the sauce. Cook a further 5 minutes.

* Worcestershire sauce should be a kosher vegetarian version if used in a meat recipe as the ordinary variety contains anchovy.

Chef's note

This is a firm family favourite.

Italian chicken spirals

Denise Phillips

Pre-heat your oven to 200°C
Preparation time: 15mins
Cooking time: 35mins

Chicken

4 Chicken breasts – thinly sliced
and flattened
4 teaspoons Sundried Tomato
paste or Tomato purée
2 tsp Garlic, peeled and crushed
1 Aubergine,
sliced thinly lengthways
5 tbsp Olive Oil
1 Egg, for coating
8 tbsp Breadcrumbs or
Matzo meal
Salt and freshly ground
Black pepper

Basil Dressing

75g Pine nuts
2 cloves Garlic, peeled
and roughly chopped
100ml Olive oil
Large bunch of fresh Basil
Salt and freshly ground
Black pepper

Garnish

Sprigs of Basil
4 cherry tomatoes sliced

Pre-heat the grill to its highest setting. Place the aubergine slices on a baking tray. Drizzle over 3 tablespoons of olive oil and grill for 5 minutes on each side or until golden.

Place the chicken breasts on a board. If too thick, flatten them by placing between 2 sheets of non-stick baking parchment paper and gently bashing with a rolling pin.

Spread each chicken breast with sundried tomato paste, then an aubergine slice and top with a few basil leaves and a sprinkling of salt and freshly ground black pepper and crushed garlic.

Roll up firmly and secure with a cocktail stick. Brush with a little beaten egg and sprinkle with breadcrumbs or matzo meal.

Heat the remaining 2 tablespoons of olive oil. Sauté the chicken breasts for about 3 minutes on each side or until golden.

Place the spirals on a baking tray. Preheat the oven to 200°C/400°F/gas mark 6. Cook for 25-30 minutes or until thoroughly cooked.

To make the dressing, roast the pine nuts in a dry frying pan for 2-3 minutes. They will cook fast so keep an eye on them. Remove immediately and transfer to another dish. Place the pine nuts, basil and garlic in the food processor. Blitz together so that it forms a paste. Gradually add the olive oil and season to taste.

To serve the stylish way: Place the chicken spirals on a warmed plate. Drizzle over some basil dressing and garnish with sliced cherry tomatoes and sprigs of basil.

Denise Phillips is a renowned chef, food columnist and the author of 5 cookbooks with her latest, The Jewish Mama's Kitchen, which was out August 2009. Her regular and popular 'hands on' cookery classes provide inspiration and new skills plus Date On A Plate, her unique cookery classes for singles, is an excellent way of networking, cooking and meeting new people. For more information on Denise, her events, charity work, gift vouchers and cook books see www.jewishcookery.com or contact her direct on 01923 836 456.

denise's kitchen
modern jewish cookery with style

Rabbi Shisler's cholent

Rabbi Shisler

Preparation time: 15mins
Cook overnight

Cholent
A good-sized piece of
Cholent meat
Potatoes – enough for
3-4 large pieces per person
1 large Onion
3-4 large Carrots
(or lots of small ones)
1 small Parsnip
1 small Turnip
1 large Courgette
1 large Leek
Barley
1 can of Butter beans
Eggs (optional)

Seasoning
Salt – a bissel
Pepper – a bit less
Garlic powder – loads!
Beef flavouring
– amount depends, see recipe
Tomato Ketchup
– a couple of big slurps

This can be made without the meat, but is much better with a gezinta-sized piece of fleish!

Peel the potatoes and cut into largish pieces. Do not have small pieces as they will disintegrate. Peel all the other vegetables and cut up into smallish pieces. Put all in cholent pot.

If you are using meat, put it in the middle of the vegetables. If using eggs, wash thoroughly and place amongst the vegetables, (still in their shells). Put the barley and butter beans on top. Put in the seasoning – if using meat, go easy on the beef flavouring. Just about cover with boiling water, put lid on cholent pot, place in the oven on a low light until lunch the next day.

Wake up in the morning enveloped in the aroma of the Garden of Eden! Spend all morning dreaming about it and at lunchtime, sit down with a glezele mashke and a plate full of steaming hot cholent, and thank the Lord for making you a Jew!

Glossary:

Glezele mashke = little glass of whisky

Gezinta = giant

Fleish = meat

Bissel = bit

With best wishes from Anne and Rabbi Geoffrey Shisler

Boeuf carbonnade

Andrew Douglas, Deputy Head,
City of London School for Girls

Pre-heat your oven to 180°C
Preparation time: 20mins
Cooking time: 2hours

2 large Onions
1 tbsp Sugar
200g Flour
1 tbsp dried Thyme
Salt and pepper to taste
As much Garlic as you like
1.5kg good diced Stewing beef
100g chopped fresh Parsley
1 large bottle of dark Beer
(eg Guinness,
Newcastle Brown)
About a pint of Beef/
Vegetable stock
A good dollop of Tomato purée
French bread,
cut into serving pieces
Mustard

Fry the onions and garlic in olive oil with the sugar and some salt until soft in a large casserole dish. Plunge the pieces of beef into a mixture of flour and dried thyme and brown them in the casserole dish. Pour in the beer and the beef stock.

Cook for about 2 hours at 180°C until the meat is well cooked and tender.

Meanwhile spread mustard on both sides of the French bread. About 15 minutes before the beef is finished, put a layer of mustardy bread croutons on top of the stew.

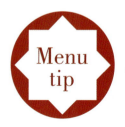

Menu
tip

Serve with the same beer you have used for cooking to drink, and with new potatoes or mash and other vegetables of your choice. Carrots are good, or else a salad of Belgian endives.

Catalan chicken

Denise Lux

Pre-heat your oven to 180°C
Preparation time: 20mins
Cooking time: 40mins

60ml Olive oil
125kg Chicken (4 pieces)
1 Onion, chopped
25kg Pine kernels
2 Tomatoes, peeled & chopped
5ml ground Cinnamon
115kg ready to eat Prunes
115ml dry White Wine
225 Chicken stock or cube
Salt
Ground black pepper

Heat 3 tablespoons of oil in a flameproof casserole. Fry the chicken pieces turning them until brown. Remove and set aside. Add onion and fry for 10 minutes until soft. Add pine kernels and fry for a further minute.

Stir in tomatoes, cinnamon, prunes, wine, stock, salt and pepper. Return the chicken to the casserole. Bring to simmering point and cover. Cook in the oven for 30-40 minutes until the chicken is thoroughly cooked.

Here's to many hours of good cooking, Pamela and Leonard Zeff

Thai green curry

Patricia Fisher

Preparation time: 30mins

Editor's note

See opposite for a great Thai green curry paste recipe.

1-3 Birdseye red chillies (to taste)
1 stick Lemon grass
2 inch square of fresh Ginger
3 Lime leaves (optional)
2 Shallots
1 small bunch Coriander
2 tsp Thai curry paste
1 tbsp Oil
4 skinned and boned Chicken breasts
1-2 tins Coconut milk (to taste)
1 packet Pea Aubergines or 10 larger Thai Aubergines
1 Lime

Whizz chillies, lemon grass, ginger, lime leaves, shallots, coriander, curry paste and oil in a food processor or liquidise.

Fry the mixture for 5 minutes then add 1 or 2 tins of coconut milk – according to taste. Add the aubergines and simmer until soft.

Add strips of chicken from 4 chicken breasts, simmer until cooked. Add the juice of 1 lime.

Chef's note

Thai aubergines may be replaced by sliced peppers and/or frozen peas.

 # Sashinka's
Thai green curry paste

Preparation time: 10mins

15 small Green chillies
4 or 5 Cloves garlic
2 or 3 stalks Lemon grass, chopped
2 or 3 Kaffir lime leaves (fresh, or dried soaked in hot water)
2 Shallots
100g or two large bunches fresh Coriander, leaves, stalks and roots
1 inch piece of fresh root Ginger
2 tsp Coriander seeds
Peeled rind of half a Lime
1 tsp black Peppercorns
1/2 tsp Salt
Small amount of Groundnut or Peanut oil

Remove the tops from the chillies but keep the seeds. Peel the ginger and chop into chunks.

Whiz up all the ingredients in a blender or processor – start with the chillies, and then add the rest. Add just enough oil to make a paste-like consistency.

Transfer the paste into a jar, and store in the fridge for up to three weeks. Makes enough for curry to serve approximately 12.

Fast roast chicken

Dorothea Josem

Pre-heat your oven to 225°C
Preparation time: 15mins
Cooking time: 45mins

1 medium to large sized
Chicken
2 sticks of Celery, diced
1 large Carrot, diced
1 large Onion, diced
1/2 Lemon
Olive Oil

Place diced vegetables on the bottom of a baking dish. Remove the chicken legs and place chicken on top of the vegetables with the legs by the side of the chicken. Place lemon inside the chicken.

Brush chicken and drumsticks generously with the olive oil and sprinkle oil on to the vegetables.

Put in preheated hot oven and leave for 45 minutes. Do not open the oven. After 45 minutes the chicken will be cooked. Remove and cover with foil for approx 10 minutes.

Sauce for roast chicken

Maureen Gold

Preparation time: 10mins
Cooking time: 20mins

1 small Apple
1 Onion
1 oz parev Margarine
1 tbsp Flour
1 tbsp Curry powder
1 tsp Chutney
1 tsp Lemon juice
1/2 Stock (300 ml)
Salt
1 oz Sultanas (optional)
2 tsp Desiccated coconut

Peel and roughly chop the apple, peel and finely chop the onion. Fry both in the margarine until the onion is lightly browned. Stir in the flour and curry powder and cook for 1-2 minutes.

Gradually add the stock and stir continuously until the liquid boils and thickens. Add the chutney, lemon juice, coconut and salt, and the sultanas if used.

Cover and simmer gently for 20 minutes.

Chef's note

Since roast chicken can sometimes be a bit boring, this sauce is a brilliant addition.

Tarragon chicken

Derry Dinkin

Chicken breasts,
skinned and boned
Olive Oil
Carrots
Celery
Button mushrooms
Tinned chopped Tomatoes
Black pepper
White wine
Tarragon, chopped

Brown the chicken in a pan in hot olive oil.

Throw in sliced carrots and celery, whole button mushrooms, tinned chopped tomatoes, black pepper, lots of white wine and chopped tarragon.

Bring to the boil then turn down to a gentle simmer and cook until done.

Menu tip

Great with roast
potatoes or rice.

Coca-Cola chicken

Sylvia Sherwood

Preparation time: 15mins
Cooking time: 1hour

Tomato Ketchup
Apricot jam
8 Chicken pieces
Single can of Coca-Cola
(not diet)

Mix equal quantities of Tomato Ketchup and apricot jam and massage pieces of chicken with it. Set into a baking pan and leave for a while. Before placing into a hot oven, pour in a can of Coca-Cola. Bake as per normal. Eat it hot or cold.

Cheater's beef

aka: Trade secrets of a kosher Philadelphian butcher

Sylvia Sherwood

Nice, rolled joint of beef –
big as you like
Big sheet of tin foil
Whole bottle of Tomato
ketchup
Packet of Osem dried French
onion soup mix

Put the beef on the tin foil, tip the bottle of ketchup over it, empty the packet of dried soup over that (no water), wrap it up, put it in the oven and go and play bridge for a couple of hours.

It's also good cold but it never lasts that long.

Minced chicken balls in tomato sauce

Freda Kosmin

Pre-heat your oven to 180°C
Preparation time: 1hour 15mins
Cooking time: 2hours

The balls
1 lb minced Chicken
1 Onion, squeezed and grated
1 Egg
Fine Matzo Meal
A little Tomato sauce
1 tbsp Oil
Salt and pepper

The sauce
A tin of Tomatoes in juice
1 tbsp Flour
1 tbsp Oil
1 tsp dried Basil
Pepper

Place the minced chicken in a bowl and make a well in the centre. Lightly beat together the egg, onion, oil, tomato sauce and seasoning, and mix with the chicken. Add enough matzo meal to make a malleable mixture. Leave in the fridge for about an hour.

Mix the sauce ingredients together (or you could use a jar of kosher tomato sauce instead!)

Form the chicken mixture into balls. Place in the sauce and bake covered, in a moderate oven, for about 2 hours. They should be nice and tender when done.

They freeze well. I usually make a larger quantity and freeze the rest.

Note
I make these using my mother's method – a bit, enough, till it's done!

Schnitzels

Jonathan Robinson

Preparation time: 10mins
Cooking time: 5mins

8 (flat-ish) Chicken or
Turkey pieces
3 Eggs
Salt and pepper
Matzo meal for dipping
Cornflake crumbs for dipping
Curry powder (optional)
Dried parsley (optional)
Oil for frying
Flour for testing

Prepare 2 bowls: one with well beaten eggs, salt and pepper. Use one egg for every 2 or 3 pieces of schnitzel. The other bowl is a mixture of matzo meal and cornflake crumbs. Add optional seasonings.

Dip each piece of meat first in the egg, shake off excess but make sure it's well covered, then coat in a layer of crumbs.

Put a medium layer of oil in your widest meat pan, and heat it gently. To test if it is hot enough, put a spot of flower in the oil. When it bubbles, put as many schnitzels as you can comfortably fit flat in the pan.

It should take about 5 minutes to brown, then turn them over. When both sides are brown, take out & drain on kitchen roll.

Chef's
note

Danger – delicious
when hot!

Fish & Vegetarian

If you have vegetarian guests, or you're after a new Shavuot recipe, look no further. Try our array of tortillas, omelettes, risottos, flans, tagines, quiches and patties. And if you're making a fish meal, there are plenty of tasty additions to the usual salmon fare.

Butternut squash risotto

Irene Leeman

Preparation time: 40mins

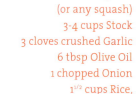

1 lb Butternut Squash
(or any squash)
3-4 cups Stock
3 cloves crushed Garlic
6 tbsp Olive Oil
1 chopped Onion
1½ cups Rice,
Arborio is best for this
Sage
1½ cups dry White Wine
(optional)
Pinch Nutmeg
Fresh ground Pepper
1 cup grated strong Cheddar

Boil the stock and simmer – reserve to one side.
(If not using wine, adjust the amount of stock accordingly.)

In a large saucepan, add diced squash and onion to warm olive oil and sauté until soft. Raise the heat to medium-high and add the rice. Stir, cook until the rice is opaque, 3-5 minutes. Add the sage. Pour in wine and stir until wine is absorbed. Add hot stock about half a cup at a time, stirring until all the stock is absorbed before adding more. Stir constantly until rice is firm and centres of kernels are no longer white – 20-25 minutes.

Stir in crushed garlic, nutmeg, salt and pepper to taste. Add more stock if necessary. Stir in cheese to taste.

Spoon the risotto into warmed plates. Add more cheese on top if wanted.

One pan salmon and roast asparagus

Jonathan Robinson

Pre-heat your oven to 220°C
(200°C for fan ovens)
Preparation time: 10mins
Cooking time: 50mins

800g New Potatoes
(halved if large)
16 Asparagus spears
4 handfuls Cherry Tomatoes
2 tbsp Olive Oil
1 tbsp Balsamic Vinegar
4 Salmon fillets (140g each)
Handful of Basil leaves

Tip the potatoes and a tablespoon of olive oil into an ovenproof dish, then roast for 20 minutes until they start to brown.

Toss the asparagus in with the potatoes, then return the dish to the oven for 15 minutes.

Throw in the cherry tomatoes and vinegar and nestle the salmon amongst the vegetables. Drizzle with the remaining oil and return to the oven for 10-15 minutes until the salmon is cooked.

Scatter over the basil leaves and serve everything scooped straight from the dish.

Fish & Vegetarian

Melanzana parmigiana
(aubergine casserole)

Bencie Woll

Pre-heat your oven to 190°C
Preparation time: 40mins
Cooking time: 30mins

1 large Aubergine
Coarse salt
1 Egg
Matzo Meal
Oil
400-600g Tomato sauce
Mozzarella

Slice the aubergine into thin slices lengthwise. Sprinkle with coarse salt and leave for 30 minutes. Rinse and pat dry.

Dip each slice in beaten egg and then in matzo meal. Fry in shallow oil until brown on both sides.

Cover the bottom of a baking dish with a thin layer of tomato sauce. Put a single layer of aubergine in the baking dish and cover with half the tomato sauce. Add a second layer of aubergine and the remainder of the sauce. Cover with mozzarella slices. Bake for 30 minutes at 190°C.

Chef's note
A great Pesach dish!

Courgette patties

Irene Leeman

Preparation time: 25mins

4 cups grated Courgettes
4 Eggs, separated
1 cup crumbled Feta cheese or grated mature Cheddar
1/2 cup grated Onions
3/4 tsp of dried Mint
Pinch salt and black pepper to taste
1/3 cup Flour

Put grated courgettes in a colander in a bowl. Let it stand for approximately 10 minutes. Then rinse and squeeze out all excess water.

Combine the eggs, cheese, onions, courgettes, flour and spices. Mix well.

Beat the egg whites till they form soft peaks and fold into the mixture. Make into patties and fry each one on both sides until brown and crisp.

Optional

Serve with sour cream or yogurt. They are nice hot or cold.

Red pepper potato tortilla

Denise Phillips

Preparation time: 35mins

XXXXXXXXXXXXXXXXX

450g Baby New Potatoes, peeled and thinly sliced
1 Spanish Onion, peeled
1 red pepper, cored and roughly chopped
3 tbsp Olive oil
4 Eggs
Salt
Freshly ground black pepper

Garnish
Sprigs of flat leaf Parsley

This is a classic Spanish dish that is similar to an omelette, but it is made with thinly sliced potatoes and onions and other store cupboard ingredients. I like to add some chopped red pepper for both colour and flavour. To ease the task of chopping the potatoes, slicing them in a magimix speeds up the preparation. It is parev and also suitable for Passover so keep the recipe for next year.

It can be served for breakfast; lunch or dinner, an excuse to make it is not required. If you are making it to serve as part of a tapas meal, I like to cut it up into wedges to serve hot from the pan.

Slice the onion into rings. Heat 2 tablespoons of the olive oil into a 20cm heavy based frying pan. Add the sliced potatoes and the onions and cook over a low heat for about 20 minutes until the potatoes are just tender. Remove from the heat.

In a large bowl, whisk the eggs together. Season well.
Add the chopped red pepper, cooked potatoes and onions.

XXXXXXXXXXXXXXXX

To serve the stylish way

Serve warm garnished with sprigs of parsley.

Heat the remaining tablespoon of olive oil in the frying pan. Pour in the potato mixture. Cook gently for 5-8 minutes until the mixture is almost set.

Place a large plate upside over the pan, invert the tortilla on to the plate and then slide it back into the pan. Cook for a final 2-3 minutes until the underside is golden brown. Slide out of the pan onto a chopping board and cut into wedges.

denise's kitchen
modern jewish cookery with style

Paul's salmon fillets
on a bed of spinach and watercress
Toni Nagel

Preparation time: 25mins
Cooking time: 30mins

6 skinned Salmon centre fillets
1 bag Baby Spinach
1 bag Watercress
2 punnets of seriously ripe,
best you can buy, Tomatoes
1 small tub Double Cream
1/2 pack Butter

Chef's note

If you can get wild salmon
so much the better – it's
worth it. Buy the tomatoes
a week before you need
them for best results. They
should be past their sell
by date ideally.

Whizz the tomatoes in a blender and strain through a sieve. Put strained 'juice' into a saucepan. Add cubed butter. Leave to one side. Blanch the spinach and watercress in boiling water for 30 seconds. Plunge into cold water. Squeeze all water from the leaves and stick in a second pan, with the cream. Leave to one side.

Using a large frying pan, sauté the salmon fillets for around 2 minutes on each side. Do not overcook! (You want them a bit underdone in the middle or else they go horribly dry.)

As you put the fish in the pan, begin to warm up the tomato sauce. Whisk the butter into the sauce. Keep warming and bring to the boil and then turn off. At the same time as the tomato sauce is heating up, start heating the spinach and cream until it is nice and hot.

Take 6 hot plates. In the middle of each plate stick 1/6 of the spinach/cream mix. Put the just cooked salmon fillet on top. Spoon the tomato sauce around the fish and serve with a vegetable of choice!

Cassoulet of butter beans

Hassan Dervish, chef to Steven Wolfisz

1 tin Butter beans
4 oz Shallots
2 cloves Garlic
4 oz chopped Tomatoes
1/2 jar Tomato sauce

Boil the butter beans until soft (to breaking point).

Chop and sauté the shallots and garlic. Add the chopped tomatoes and tomato sauce. Drain the beans and mix with the sauce. Heat the mixture until it becomes 'stodgy'.

Chef's note

Serve garnished with chopped coriander.

Gefilte fish

Frankie Abramson

Cooking time: 30mins

Stock
Cold water
1 large Onion
3 Carrots
2 heaped tbsp white Sugar
1 level tbsp Salt
1 tsp Pepper
1 or 2 Salmon heads
2 Salmon backbones

Fish balls
2 lb filleted skinned Haddock
1 Onion
2 tbsp Virgin Olive Oil
2 heaped tsp Sugar
Salt and White pepper to taste
4 tbsp ground Almonds

Half fill a 12 inch saucepan with cold water. Add a quartered onion and sliced carrots, as well as the sugar, salt and pepper. Add the fish heads and backbones. Bring to the boil and simmer for one hour, then carefully remove the fish heads and bones – beware, they disintegrate!

While the stock is boiling, prepare the fish. Cut haddock into chunks and combine with chopped onion. Mince the mixture in a blender so that the fish has a 'chopped' consistency. Place mixture in a large bowl, adding all other fish ball ingredients and mixing thoroughly. Roll the mixture into balls – it should make around 15.

Gently place the balls into the hot stock and bring back to the boil. Simmer for 90 minutes. Decorate with carrot slices.

Chef's note

As an alternative to boiling in stock, the fish balls can be fried in a pan filled 2/3 full with oil. Flatten the balls slightly first. Cook for 15-20 minutes, turning intermittently. Remove, and place to dry on a plate lined with kitchen roll.

Leek patties

Debbie Talalay

1 small raw Onion
2 lbs Leeks, cooked
2 Eggs
4 heaped tbsp medium Matzo Meal
Salt
Plenty of pepper
Pinch of Cayenne pepper

Steam or boil the leeks until tender. Drain and press excess liquid out.

Mince the leeks and onions then mix with the other ingredients. If the mixture is too loose, add more matzo meal. If it is too dry, add more egg. Allow the mixture to cool then form into small patties in palm of the hand.

Fry in hot oil for 5 minutes on each side.

Squeeze a lemon over the patties before serving.

Chef's note

If there are any left the following day – which is most unlikely – they are delicious cold.

" *With best wishes from all the Talalay family* "

Spinach omelette

Fariba Schmetterling

One bag of Spinach
(300 to 400g)
1 tsp Salt
1 tsp Pepper
1 tsp Turmeric
1 tsp Cumin (all spices to taste)
6 Eggs
Vegetable or Olive Oil

Put the washed spinach in a big bowl and add the salt and spices, then break the eggs on top and mix well.

In a large pan heat some oil with a bit of turmeric added. When hot, pour the mixture into the pan and fry on a low temperature until the bottom of the omelette is nice and crispy, then turn over using a big plate or round tray and cook the other side for about 8-10 minutes longer or until crispy.

Leave to settle for 5 minutes and then move to a large plate and cut into portions. Serve hot with bread or matzo and some plain yogurt, or with bread and salad or even pickle, according to your taste.

> 66
>
> *"Happy cooking! Fariba, Dori and*
> *Raphael Schmetterling*
> *Keep your valuable data secure with*
> *our online backup service*
> ***www.schmetterlingbackup.com"***
>
> 99

Stuffed lentil roast

Sandra Blackman

Pre-heat your oven to 180°C
Preparation time: 25mins
Cooking time: 45mins

Loaf
1 tbsp Oil
2 chopped Onions
2 Tomatoes
1 Apple
8 oz Lentils
1/2 tsp flavouring
1/2 tsp Coriander
2 oz Oats
1 Egg
Salt
Pepper

Stuffing
1/2 tbsp Oil
8 oz Mushrooms
2 Tomatoes
2 oz Oats
2 tbsp Parlsey
1 tbsp Chives

Chop the tomatoes, peel and grate the apple.

Heat oil in a large saucepan. Add the tomatoes and apple. Sweat for few minutes. Add the lentils and water to just cover. Add the flavouring and cook until the lentils are done. Add the oats, egg and seasoning.

Prepare the stuffing: Heat oil and toss in chopped mushrooms, tomatoes and herbs.

Spoon half the lentil mix into a greased loaf tin or deep dish. Top with the stuffing. Add the rest of the lentil mix.

Bake at 180°C for 45 minutes.

" *"Happy, healthy eating – Sandra"* "

Grilled fillet of mackerel

Edwina Brown

Preparation time: 5mins
Cooking time: 5mins

4 Mackerel fillets,
bones removed
1 tbsp Olive oil
2 tsp squeezed Lemon juice
Sea salt
Freshly ground black pepper
Almonds (optional)

Pre-heat the grill on full power. Score the skins of the mackerel fillets lightly to assist even cooking and avoid the fillets curling up. Season the fillets lightly with sea salt and freshly ground black pepper and place, skin side up, onto a baking tray. Position under a hot grill for 4-5 minutes depending on the thickness of the fillets, then remove from the grill and squeeze a little fresh lemon juice over them.

For an optional extra, roast almonds in a hot oven (180°C) for 8 minutes and sprinkle over the top.

For a delicious meal, dish up a helping of the tagine of winter root vegetables (see opposite page), add some chopped coriander and lemon juice, lay a grilled mackerel fillet on top, sprinkle with the toasted almonds and serve with roasted garlic.

Tagine of winter root vegetables with chickpeas

Edwina Brown

Pre-heat your oven to 180°C
Preparation time: 50mins
Cooking time: 1hour

Menu tip

See opposite for a fantastic meal idea with grilled mackerel.

2 cloves Garlic
Olive Oil
8 large vine ripened Plum Tomatoes
Sea salt
Freshly ground black pepper
Pinch of Sugar
1 tsp fresh Ginger
1 small Onion
1/4 Butternut Squash
2 sticks Celery
1 medium Carrot
1 medium Courgette
2 tbsp Olive Oil
Spice mix (see note)
1 stick Cinnamon
150g chickpeas, dried and soaked in cold water overnight

Pre-heat the oven to 180°C. Crush the garlic and chop the tomatoes roughly. In a medium saucepan on a medium heat soften the garlic in olive oil for 2 minutes with no colour. Add the chopped tomatoes, bring to a simmer, season with salt and black pepper and cook with a bubble just breaking the surface for 30 minutes. Pass through a sieve, taste and adjust the seasoning if required. Reserve to one side.

Chop the ginger, onion, butternut squash, celery, carrot and courgette. In a large saucepan, on a medium heat, soften the vegetables with the spices in olive oil for 6 minutes. Add the soaked chickpeas and the tomato fondue prepared earlier, bring to a simmer, season with salt and freshly ground black pepper, cover with a lid and cook with a bubble just breaking the surface for 1 hour.

Spice mix

1/4 tsp ground anise, 1 tsp ground turmeric, 1/4 tsp cayenne pepper, 1/4 tsp ground cardamom, 1/4 tsp ground coriander seeds, 1/4 tsp ground cumin, 1/4 tsp ground black pepper

Potato flan with mushrooms and peppers

Denise Levy

Pre-heat your oven to 170°C
Preparation time: 25mins
Cooking time: 35mins

1 lb Potatoes
knob of Margarine
2 tbsp Milk
2 tbsp Vegetable Oil
1 small Onion
4 oz Mushroom
1 Red Pepper
1 Egg
1/4 pint Milk
2 oz grated Cheddar
Salt and pepper

Cube the potatoes and cook in boiling water for 10-15 minutes until tender. Drain well and mash with the margarine, 2 tablespoons of milk and a little seasoning.

Meanwhile, heat the oil in a large frying pan, add the chopped pepper, onion and mushrooms and cook gently for about 8 minutes until softened and beginning to brown. Season well to taste.

Preheat the oven to 170°C. Brush a small heatproof dish with oil. Using your fingers, press the mashed potato mixture into the dish until the base and sides are evenly covered. Transfer the vegetables into the potato case.

Beat together the 1/4 pint of milk, egg and a little seasoning. Pour over the vegetables and top with grated cheese. Bake for 25-35 minutes until set.

Salmon fillets with salsa verde

Marcia Goodman

Pre-heat your oven to 180°C
Preparation time: 35mins
Cook time: 25mins

2 handfuls Flat Leaf Parsley
10 Basil leaves
10 fresh Mint leaves
1 clove Garlic, crushed
1 tbsp Dijon mustard
1 tbsp Capers, drained
2 Anchovy fillets
1/2 tsp Red Wine Vinegar
150 ml Olive Oil
Salmon fillets

Crush the garlic and drain the capers. Place the parsley, mint, basil, garlic, mustard, capers, anchovy, vinegar and oil in a processor and purée. Add salt and pepper to taste. Cover and let stand for about 30 minutes.

Place salmon fillets in a greased baking dish and cover with the salsa. Cook for 25 minutes at 180°C.

" "

"Wishing the Guild every success with the cookery book, Julian and Judy Machet"

, ,

Russian jewel latkes

Sharlott Toube

Preparation time: 25mins

5 Eggs
5 oz plumped,
colourful Dried Fruit
8 fl oz sieved Cottage Cheese
8 fl oz Sour Cream
or Greek Yogurt
A few drops of Vanilla or
Almond flavouring
1 tsp grated Orange or
Lemon zest
4¹ᐟ² oz Flour
1 tbsp Sugar
1¹ᐟ² tsp Baking Powder
Pinch of salt
Pinch of ground Nutmeg or
mixed Spice

Whisk together the eggs, dried fruit, cottage cheese, sour cream or yogurt, flavouring and zest. Sift together the flour, sugar, baking powder, salt and spices. Fold the dry mixture into the liquids.

Fry twenty 3 inch diameter pancakes in batches in a mixture of butter and oil and serve with more sour cream or crème fraîche and cinnamon sugar to taste.

Chef's note

This is a wonderful Chanukah recipe that also works well on Shavuot.

No pastry quiche

Denise Levy

Pre-heat your oven to 170°C
Preparation time: 20mins
Cooking time: 40mins

2 tbsp Vegetable Oil
1 large Onion
1 clove Garlic
12 oz Leeks
4 oz Courgettes
4 oz Mushrooms
1-2 Red Peppers
1 Green Pepper
2 Eggs
1/3 pint Milk
Chopped Parsley
4 oz grated Cheddar
Salt and pepper
2 Tomatoes

Heat the oil in a large frying pan, add crushed garlic and chopped onion and fry gently for a few minutes. Add chopped leeks, courgettes and mushrooms and fry gently until softened. Add chopped peppers. Transfer the mixture to a lightly greased 25cm flan dish.

In a bowl, whisk the eggs with the milk, stir in the parsley, seasoning and most of the cheese. Pour the mixture over the vegetables and arrange sliced tomatoes on top. Sprinkle over the remaining cheese. Bake, uncovered, in the preheated oven for 35-40 minutes until firm and lightly browned.

66

*"With best wishes from
Mirco Keilflug"*

99

Salads & Sides

We have gathered together our favourite salad and side dish recipes to enhance your Shabbat meals and dinner parties. Some of these, like the gravadlax and green lentil salad, are also fantastic as starters – look out for the chefs' notes to see which ones.

Cobb salad

Maxine Margolis

Preparation time: 25mins

Salad
2 Romaine Lettuces
4 hard-boiled Eggs
4 Rosa Tomatoes
2 English Cucumbers
2 Avocados
8-10 Sundried Tomatoes
125g Calamata Olives
Croutons

Dressing
1/4 Red Onion, finely chopped
1 stick Celery
2 tsp Dijon Mustard
1 tsp Mustard powder
3 tsp Balsamic Vinegar
3 tsp Apple Cider Vinegar
2/3 cup Olive Oil
2 tsp Sugar
1 pinch Paprika
Coarse salt & black pepper

Slice the lettuce coarsely and mound onto a platter. Dice the cucumbers, tomatoes and avocados. Separate the boiled egg yolks and whites and chop them separately. Arrange them apart on top of the lettuce in rows with the other vegetables and croutons.

Place the dressing ingredients in a liquidiser and blend until well mixed. Dress only just before serving.

Tip

Dressing can be made ahead & refrigerated.

Red cabbage salad

Joyce King

Preparation time: 15mins
Chilling time: 1hour

◆ ◆ ◆ ◆ ◆ ◆ ◆

Salad
1 lb Red Cabbage
1/3 cup Spring Onion
1/3 cup Pine Nuts
3 cups grated Carrots
1 small can Mandarins
(reserve juice)
1-2 handfuls dried Cranberries

Dressing
4 tbsp Brown Sugar, to taste
4 tbsp Red Wine vinegar
1 tbsp Mandarin juice
1/2 cup Oil
1 tsp (parev) Chicken flavour
soup powder
1/2 tsp Garlic powder
Salt and black pepper

Shred the red cabbage and chop the spring onion.

Mix salad ingredients together in a bowl. Whisk dressing ingredients together.

Mix with the salad and refrigerate for at least one hour.

The Sharron family
are delighted to
sponsor the NWES
Guild Cookery Book

Bang bang chicken salad

Tony Page

Preparation time: 10mins
Cooking time: 10mins

2 skinless Chicken breasts
1 pint of fresh Chicken stock
1 inch of fresh Ginger,
peeled and sliced
1 tbsp smooth Peanut Butter
1 tbsp clear Honey
1 tbsp Sesame Oil
1 tsp Chilli Oil
1/2 Cucumber,
cut into matchsticks
2 Carrots, cut into matchsticks
4 Spring Onions,
cut into matchsticks
1/2 Iceberg Lettuce,
shredded or thinly sliced
1 bunch of Coriander
Handful of Sesame Seeds
A pinch Paprika
Coarse salt
Black pepper

Pour the stock into a saucepan, add the ginger and bring to the boil. Once the stock has come to a boil, add the chicken breasts and gently simmer for about 10 minutes or until cooked.

Remove the chicken from the stock, reserving the stock for the dressing and allow the chicken to cool.

Place 6 teaspoons of the (cooled) reserved stock into a jar, adding the peanut butter, honey, sesame oil and chilli oil. Shake well to mix.

Put the lettuce together with the carrots and cucumber into four serving dishes. Shred the chicken and place on top of the vegetables. Drizzle with the sauce and garnish with a handful of fresh coriander and sesame seeds.

www.tonypage.com
info@tonypage.com
Tel: 020 8830 4000

Cucumber salad

Anne Shisler

Preparation time: 30mins

1 Cucumber
1 tub natural yogurt
2 tsp Wine Vinegar
Pepper
2 tsp Lemon juice
2 tsp Sugar
a pinch of Salt
2 tsp chopped Parsley
(optional)

Using a potato peeler make stripes down the side of the cucumber, slice thinly. Sprinkle with salt and weight with a plate to press out liquid.

Drain off liquid after about 30 minutes. Put into a serving dish.

Beat the yogurt with the remaining ingredients and pour over the cucumber. Refrigerate until required and serve cold.

Apricot salad

Anne Shisler

3-4 oz Dried Apricots
1 oz Sultanas or Raisins
Orange juice
1 eating Apple
1 tbsp Lemon juice
1 small White or Red Cabbage
2 sticks Celery

Chop the cabbage, celery, apple and dried apricots.

Soak the apricots and sultanas in orange juice, enough to cover, for about half an hour. Toss the chopped apple in the lemon juice.

Mix all the ingredients together. Add a bit more orange juice to make sure the salad is not dry.

Chef's note:

High in fibre and healthy!

Rabbi Shaul's turkey salad

Rabbi Shaul Robinson

1 large Turkey drumstick
finely chopped Celery
1 Red Pepper
1 Orange Pepper
Mayonnaise
Roasted Almonds or Cashews
Paprika

Roast the turkey drumstick, leave to cool.

Then chop up and mix all ingredients with mayonnaise, and add a dash of paprika.

Fried plantains

Bobo Bergstrom

Preparation time: 25mins

Plantains
Oil
White and Red Onions
Chives
Red Peppers
Garlic cloves

Use half-ripe plantains (yellow but not too much black). Peel and cut the plantains into 5mm slices on a bias. Deep-fry them or pan-fry them until golden brown.

Sauté finely sliced white and red onion, chives, red pepper and garlic in a good bit of oil and top the plantain with this seasoning before serving.

Chef's note

If you use a plantain that is too ripe there will not be enough starch to keep the texture when you fry them.

Apple or pear chutney

Linda Brody

Preparation time: 2 weeks

2 lbs Apples or Pears	Core the fruit but do not peel. Chop fruit, onions and pepper and simmer in a pan with the vinegar until soft. Add sugar. Place spices in a muslin bag and add. Leave to stand for 4 or 5 hours.
1 lb Onions	
1 Red Pepper	
3/4 lb Sugar	
1/2 pt Vinegar	Slow boil again and stir regularly. Remove muslin bag, cool and pour into warm, sterilised jars.
Pickling spices	

Leave to mature for 2 weeks before consuming.

Dear friends, enjoy and may the New West End Synagogue Guild continue their wonderful work. Your chavera from the Netherlands, Dora Boom

Gravadlax and green lentil salad

Denise Phillips

Preparation time: 10mins
Cooking time: 40mins

◆ ◆ ◆ ◆ ◆ ◆ ◆

200g Puy Green Lentils
1 Red Onion,
peeled and finely chopped
1 tbsp White Wine Vinegar
2 tbsp Extra Virgin Olive Oil
6 Cherry Tomatoes, cut in half
1 Beetroot bulb, ready cooked,
not in vinegar, sliced
2 tbsp fresh flat leaf Parsley,
finely chopped
2 tbsp fresh Dill,
finely chopped
2 tbsp Mustard and Dill sauce
or substitute 1 tsp Mustard and
2 tbsp Mayonnaise
300g Cured Gravadlax
50g Watercress
Salt
Freshly ground black pepper

Garnish
1 lemon – cut into wedges

◆ ◆ ◆ ◆ ◆

This salad makes a little luxury ingredient go a long way as you mix the delicious cured salmon with some nutty green lentils. It is ideal as a tasty starter or used as part of a buffet dish for Shabbat or Yom Tov.

Gravadlax originated as a way of food preservation during the time of the Middle Ages when the fishermen salted the salmon and lightly fermented it by burying it in the sand above the high-tide line.

The gravadlax comes from the Scandinavian word 'grav' which literally means 'grave' or 'hole in the ground' and 'lax' which means salmon, thus gravadlax means 'salmon dug into the ground'. Today the salmon is 'buried' in a dry marinade of salt, sugar and dill for a few days. As the salmon cures by the action of osmosis, the moisture turns the dry cure into a highly concentrated brine.

Put the lentils and onion in a pan with 750ml water. Bring to the boil and simmer for 25 minutes or until tender but not mushy.

In a bowl, mix the vinegar, mustard sauce and olive oil and season with salt and freshly ground black pepper. Drain the lentils and onion. Rinse in cold water and drain again. Add to the vinegar dressing and lightly toss. Add the tomato, herbs and beetroot.

Arrange the salmon slices on each plate and top with the lentil mixture and watercress.

To serve the stylish way:

Dust the plate with a sprinkling of black pepper and garnish with lemon wedges.

Apple horseradish

Trevor Toube

Preparation time: 15mins

1 lb Apples
2 tbsp Horseradish
4 tbsp Vinegar
2 tbsp Sugar
Salt and pepper to taste

Peel and grate the apple and grate the horseradish. Combine all ingredients.

Serve fresh with meat dishes.

Beetroot relish

Trevor Toube

Preparation time: 15mins
Overnight Cooling

4 fl oz Vinegar
1 tbsp Sugar
1 tsp Salt
1 tsp Caraway Seeds
2 tsp Horseradish
1 small Apple
2 cups cooked Beetroot

Simmer the vinegar, sugar, salt and caraway seeds for 5 minutes. Add grated horseradish, peeled and diced apple and sliced beetroot.

Remove from the heat and refrigerate overnight.

Peperonata

Marcia Goodman

Preparation time: 5mins
Cooking time: 30mins

1 large Onion
1/4 pint Olive Oil
2 cloves minced Garlic
2 lbs Red Peppers
1 lb Tomatoes
Salt and pepper to taste

Slice the onions thinly and slice the peppers into strips. Cook the onions gently in the oil. After the onions have become translucent add the garlic and pepper strips.

Cover and cook very slowly for about 15 minutes. Add the chopped tomatoes and cook for another 15 minutes. Season.

Cool before serving.

Chef's note

This is my version of a very good Southern French dish. Delicious as a starter with crusty bread.

Stuffed mushrooms

Sheli Rodney

Pre-heat your oven to 180°C
Preparation time: 10mins
Cooking time: 30mins

Chef's note:

Also great as
a starter.

6 large Portobello Mushrooms,
with good rim to allow
for stuffing
1 pack Cherry Tomatoes
1 pack fresh Spinach
Garlic salt to taste
Black pepper to taste
Soy sauce

Lay out the mushrooms on an oven-proof tray.

Chop the cherry tomatoes into halves. Press 3 or 4 halves face down into each mushroom cup, depending how many will fit around the stem. If half tomatoes are too wide to squeeze into the mushroom between the rim and the stem, try cutting them into quarters instead. Wash a handful of spinach. Scrunch a few leaves and wedge them between the tomato pieces, until each mushroom is stuffed full.

Sprinkle some garlic salt and black pepper over the top of each mushroom. Then carefully pour about a tablespoon of soy sauce into each mushroom, allowing it to drizzle down between the stuffing.

Cover tray with tin foil and bake for at least 30 minutes, the longer the better. Serve one or two each as a side dish.

Spinach salad

Maxine Margolis

Preparation time: 15mins

◆ ◆ ◆ ◆ ◆ ◆ ◆

Salad
2 Packets Baby Spinach
1 Avocado
1 punnet Strawberries
or 2 Mangos
1 small bunch
Baby Spring Onions
2 packets crushed
Caramelised Nuts

Dressing
4 tbsp Balsamic Vinegar
1/2 cup of Salad Oil
1/2 cup of Olive Oil
1 tsp Salt
2 tbsp Lemon juice
2 tsp Dry Mustard
2 tbsp Brown sugar (or white)

Place cut up avocado and halved strawberries (or cut up mangos) on a bed of spinach mixed with the chopped spring onions.

Sprinkle over the crushed nuts.

Whisk dressing ingredients together in a liquidiser or food processor and pour over the salad before serving.

ENJOY!
Best wishes from
Marcella Spelman

Sauté spinach with pine nuts and raisins

Silvia Nacamulli

Preparation time: 20mins

1kg fresh Spinach leaves
4-5 tbsp Extra Virgin Olive Oil
1 finely chopped Onion
a handful of Raisins
a handful of Pine Nuts
Salt and freshly ground black pepper to taste

cooking for the soul...

Wash the spinach well and without draining it, put it in a deep saucepan, cover and leave it to steam with a tablespoon of sea salt for 5-7 minutes.

Once the spinach is tender, drain it, leave it to cool down and squeeze the water out. In the meantime, heat up the olive oil and the chopped onion in a frying pan with some salt and pepper. Leave to cook, stirring occasionally, for 5 minutes until the onion is soft. To help in the process, add a few tablespoons of warm water and leave it to evaporate. Once the water has evaporated and the onion starts to turn golden, add the steamed and squeezed spinach, stir well and leave to cook for 10 minutes.

Soak the raisins in water for a few minutes, and let them become soft and juicy. Add them to the spinach together with the pine nuts and leave to sauté for another few minutes. Serve warm or at room temperature.

Chef's note

You don't need to add any additional water when steaming the spinach, as it will release its own liquid while cooking.

Traditional potato kugel

Shana Ballon

Pre-heat your oven to 180°C
Preparation time: 20mins
Cooking time: 1¼hours

6 medium Potatoes
1 Onion
2 medium Carrots, grated (optional)
3 large Eggs, beaten
1/3 cup Flour or medium Matzo Meal
1$^{1/2}$ tsp Salt
1/4 tsp fresh ground Black pepper
4 tbsp Vegetable Oil
1/4 tsp Baking Powder

Peel potatoes and place in bowl of cold water. Grate onion (small to medium holes) into a large bowl. Grate potatoes one at a time on medium holes and combine with the onion. Add eggs and mix. Stir in remaining ingredients and combine well using a fork.

Place in greased 9 x 9 inch baking pan and bake for at least 1$^{1/4}$ hours or until top is light golden brown and crisp.

This recipe freezes wonderfully.

 # Moravian cabbage

Erica Wyld

Preparation time: 30mins

1¹ᐟ² lbs shredded White Cabbage
1 cup Water
1 medium Onion
1/2 cup Chicken fat or similar
1/3 cup Flour
1/2 tsp Caraway Seeds
Salt to taste
4 tsp Sugar
1/3 cup Vinegar

Simmer the cabbage in water for 5 minutes. Brown the onion in chicken fat, add flour and stir until brown.

Pour in the liquid from the cabbage and stir until smooth.

Add cabbage, caraway seeds, salt, sugar and vinegar. Simmer for 20 minutes.

May this book be to every recipient's taste and benefit each charity donation. Best wishes, Barbara and Roy Levin.

Broccoli kugel

Tina Son

Pre-heat your oven to 180°C
Preparation time: 20mins
Cooking time: 40mins

1 bag frozen Broccoli
1/2 bag frozen chopped Spinach
1 Egg
1 tbsp Mayonnaise
A little Self-raising Flour

Season broccoli and spinach and cook over a medium heat on the hob until broccoli is soft. Do not add any water. When soft, strain as much excess liquid as possible.

Mash broccoli and spinach until you have a smooth mixture. Add beaten egg and mayonnaise. Stir in a little flour to absorb any excess fluid. Turn into a greased baking dish and bake in oven at 180°C for 40 minutes.

Fried-over cauliflower

Tina Son

Preparation time: 15mins

1 bag frozen Cauliflower
1 large Onion
1 Egg
1 cup medium Matzo Meal
Sunflower Oil

Season the cauliflower and boil until soft. Chop and fry the onion.

Mix the onion and cauliflower together, add beaten egg and matzo meal. Fry the cauliflower and onion mix in sunflower oil until a little brown.

Tip:

Can be cooked in advance & reheated in a microwave.

Vegetable kugel

Anne Shisler

Preparation time: 20mins
Cooking time: 1-1¼hours

◆ ◆ ◆ ◆ ◆ ◆ ◆

3 large Courgettes
3 large Carrots
2 baking Potatoes
1 large Onion
4 Eggs
1¹/² tsp Salt
Black pepper
150ml Sunflower Oil
125g Matzo Meal
50g Breadcrumbs

Peel potatoes and then grate all the vegetables finely.

Whisk the eggs with the seasonings until fluffy, and add the oil, meal, breadcrumbs and then the vegetables.

Mix well and pour into a greased dish. Bake for 1-1¼ hours until a rich golden brown.

◆ ◆ ◆ ◆ ◆ ◆ ◆

Chef Bobo's Caribbean sweet potato salad

Bobo Bergstrom

◆ ◆ ◆ ◆ ◆ ◆

3 Sweet Potatoes
1/2 Cucumber, peeled, seeded and sliced in an angle
1 small Red Onion, in wedges
1 – 2 Spring Onions
1 Red Sweet Pepper, sliced
Hot pepper

Dressing
2 Egg yolks
2 tsp Vinegar
1$^{1/2}$ tbsp Turmeric
1 tbsp Brown Sugar
1-2 tsp. fresh Ginger, grated
1 tbsp Kosher Dijon or mild Mustard
$^{1/2}$ tsp hot Chilli sauce
3/4 cup Cooking Oil
1/4 cup Olive Oil
2 tsp Lime juice
1 tsp Brown Mustard Seeds

Whisk egg yolks, sugar, turmeric, vinegar and mustard to smooth consistency, thicken with the oil as with a mayonnaise and season with hot sauce, mustard seeds, lime juice and salt.

Peel and cut the sweet potato into 1 inch cubes, then cook in salted water with some turmeric for a few minutes until they still have crispy consistency, "al dente". Strain and set aside in a large salad bowl.

Sauté the rest of the vegetables in olive oil and add to the potatoes, toss with the dressing and serve directly lukewarm or at room temperature.

Chef's note

Kosher chilli sauces or Habenero sauces are easily available. If you don't like chilli leave out the hot pepper and chilli sauce.

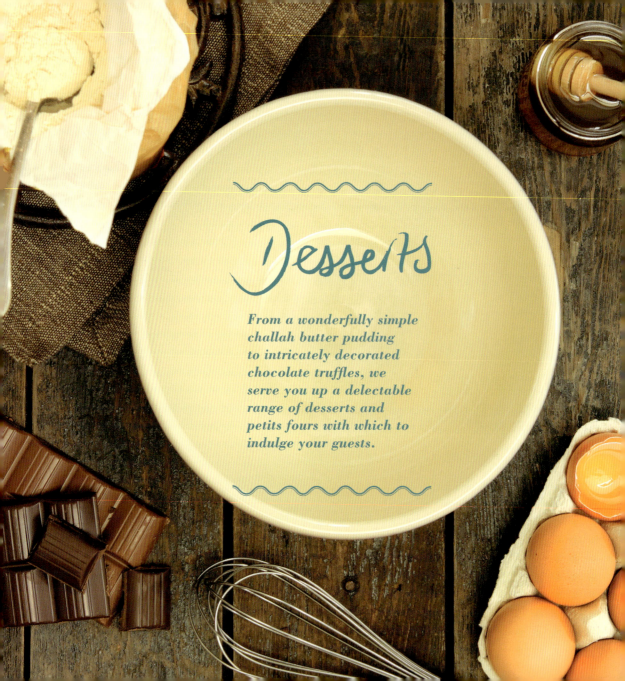

Desserts

From a wonderfully simple challah butter pudding to intricately decorated chocolate truffles, we serve you up a delectable range of desserts and petits fours with which to indulge your guests.

Boozy banana fritters

Sharlott Toube

Preparation time: 20mins

2 oz Flour
1/4 tsp Baking Powder
1 Egg yolk
1 tbsp Oil
4 fl oz Beer
1 Egg white
Pinch of salt
Bananas

Sift the flour and baking powder. Beat well with the egg yolk, oil and beer. Set aside in a warm place for an hour. Then fold in one egg white, beaten until stiff with a pinch of salt.

Peel and cut chunks of ripe banana, roll them in flour, dip into the batter and deep-fry.

Serve immediately!

Serving tip

Try either dredged with sugar or flambéed with brandy or rum.

Oranges orientales

Hilde Matheson

B'tayavon –
Hilde Matheson

Preparation time: 15mins
Cooking time: 40mins

8 large Oranges
$1^{1/2}$ cups Sugar
$1^{1/2}$ cups Golden Syrup
1/4 cup Lemon juice
1/2 cup Cointreau

Remove the peel from 4 oranges, making sure all white membrane is removed. Cut the peel into match-like strips – I use an orange zester. Place peel in a small saucepan with 2 cups of water and bring to the boil covered. Remove from the heat, drain and set aside.

Peel the other 4 oranges and cut all oranges into circles or leave whole, if preferred, and place in an ovenproof dish.

In a large saucepan, combine sugar, golden syrup and $1^{1/2}$ cups of water. Bring to the boil over a high flame, stirring all the time, until the sugar has dissolved. Cook uncovered over medium heat for 10 minutes. Add the reserved peel and continue to cook for 30 minutes longer – or until the syrup is slightly thickened. Remove from the heat and add lemon juice and Cointreau. Pour this hot syrup over the oranges.

Allow to cool and refrigerate, covered, for at least 8 hours. If you have left the oranges whole, turn them occasionally in the syrup. This desert keeps well in the fridge and can be served with vanilla ice-cream.

Malva pudding

Maxine Margolis

Pre-heat your oven to 160°C
Preparation time: 15mins
Cooking time: 45mins

~~~~~~~~~~~~~~~~~~~

Pudding
1 Egg
15ml Apricot jam
5ml Bicarbonate of soda
15ml Butter
250ml Milk
250g Sugar
250g Flour
Salt
5ml Vinegar

Sauce
125ml Milk
250ml Sugar
125ml Butter
125ml Cream
125ml hot Water

Sift the flour with bicarbonate of soda.

Beat egg and sugar in a mixer, add the jam.

Melt the vinegar and butter. Add vinegar, butter and milk to the egg mixture, alternating with the sifted flour. Beat well and bake in a buttered dish for 45 minutes at 160°C.

Melt the sauce ingredients and pour over the pudding as it comes out of the oven. Serve with whipped cream.

Best wishes from
Stanley Blum

~~~~~~~~~~~~~~~~~~~

Federico's 'simple' chocolate fondant

Toni Nagel

Pre-heat your oven to 210°C
Freezing time: 4hours

200g Chocolate
200g Sugar
100g Butter
40g Flour
6 Eggs

Put the butter and chocolate pieces in a pan and let them melt. Mix the eggs, sugar and flour in a bowl, then add the melted chocolate. Pour the whole mix into ramekins, let them freeze (approx. 4 hours.)

Bake them for about 10 minutes (until the top of the cakes are baked) when required.

Serving tip

With sour cream or pouring cream ...Mmm, delicious!

Parev chocolate sauce

Yvonne Shisler

Preparation time: 15mins

10 oz Oil
3 Eggs
3 tbsp Cocoa
10 oz Sugar
1 cup boiling Water

Place all the ingredients in a saucepan and bring to the boil. Stir to the required consistency.

Cranberry-raspberry mousse

Valerie Green

350g fresh Cranberries
350g fresh Raspberries
1 Raspberry Jelly
in 300 ml of Boiled water
2 tbsp of Granulated
or Brown sugar

Stew cranberries, lightly liquidise or mash with sugar. Liquidise or mash raspberries. Mix in jelly and whip cream, fold in fruit. Place in dish and into fridge. Can be frozen, but defrost in fridge before eating.

To serve: 300ml fresh double cream or parev cream (whipping) when serving with a meat meal

Chef's note You can use frozen fruit but make sure they've thawed first!

Halva ice cream

Dorothea Josem

Preparation time: 15mins
Freeze overnight

8-10 oz Halva
(with Pistachios)
10 fl oz Whipping Cream
3 Eggs
2 oz Caster sugar

Crumble the halva until it looks like coarse sand. Whisk the cream until it holds soft peaks. Gently fold in the halva.

Without washing the beaters, whip the eggs and sugar together until pale and increased in volume (approximately 5 minutes with electric whisk).

Fold the eggs gently into the cream mixture. Spoon the mixture into a loaf tin.

Freeze for one hour and stir, and then freeze overnight. Turn out of the tin to serve. Decorate with pistachios.

Worth all those calories! From Cyril Benjamin and Dorothea Josem

ⓓ Chocolate truffles

Trevor Toube

Preparation time: 1hour 20mins

Chef's note: If you have pesachdike brandy this makes a great Passover treat.

Truffles
50g Butter
125g Dark Chocolate
3 Egg Yolks
50g ground Toasted Nuts
2 dessert spoons Brandy

Melt and stir together the butter and chocolate. Remove from the heat and, one by one, work in the egg yolks, then the ground toasted nuts, then the brandy.

Refrigerate for an hour to firm up, before shaping the mixture into small balls which fit into tiny paper sweet cases.

Decoration
Granulated Sugar
Powdered Sugar
Cocoa Powder
Desiccated Coconut
Toasted nuts

Roll a quarter of the balls in granulated sugar, another quarter in sifted powdered sugar, the third quarter in sifted cocoa powder, and the last batch in desiccated coconut or finely chopped, toasted nuts.

You might even decorate some by pressing a piece of toasted nut into the tops of the sweets. Place in paper cases in a pretty box – for 'professional' presentation – and store in a cool larder (not the refrigerator).

Frangipane flan

Carmel Stockman

Pre-heat your oven to gas mark 5
Preparation time: 20mins
Cooking time: 40mins

Tip

This flan
freezes well.

Flan
8 oz Puff Pastry
4 tbsp Apricot jam
4 oz soft Margarine
4 oz Caster Sugar
2 Eggs
4 oz ground Almonds

Icing
2 oz Icing Sugar
1-2 tsp Boiling water

Roll out pastry and line a lightly greased 8 inch flan dish. Reserve the trimmings. Spread jam over the pastry base. Put margarine sugar, eggs and almonds in mixer and blend well. Spread mixture over the jam.

Roll out pastry trimmings into strips long enough to cross the dish and arrange them in a criss-cross fashion over the top, sealing the ends with water. Bake in a pre-heated oven for 40-45 minutes at gas mark 5, middle shelf.

Meanwhile beat icing sugar and water together to make a smooth icing. When done, remove the flan from oven, brush with the icing and return to the oven for a further 5 minutes. Can be served hot or cold. If serving hot leave to cool for 10 minutes before serving.

Challah butter pudding

Susan Katz

Pre-heat your oven to 350°F
Preparation time: 20mins
Cooking time: 40mins

6 slices Fruit Challah
2 oz softened Butter
or Tomor margarine
2 tbsp Marmalade or Jam
12 fl oz Milk or Soya Milk
3 Eggs
75g Sugar
Grated zest of 1 large Orange
1 tbsp Demerara Sugar

Lightly butter a 7 x 9 inch baking dish.

Cut the challah into 1/2 inch thick slices. Take each slice and spread one side with marmalade/jam and the other side with butter, then cut in half.

Arrange the challah in the dish buttered-side up with the slices overlapping each other.

Whisk the milk, eggs and caster sugar together until frothy and pour over the challah. Scatter the orange zest and Demerara sugar over the top.

Bake on a high shelf for 35-40 minutes at 350°F (180°C).

Sponsored
by Georgia &
Lily Katz

Fruit cocktail pudding

Pamela Hammerschlag

Pre-heat your oven to 350°F
Preparation time: 10mins
Cooking time: 35mins

~~~~~~~~~~~~~~~

Pudding
2 cups self-raising Flour
1 cup Sugar
2 tsp bicarbonate of Soda
1 tsp Salt
2 Eggs
1 tin Fruit Cocktail

Sauce
1 cup Sugar
1 tsp Vanilla essence
1/2 cup Tinned Milk
1/2 cup Desiccated Coconut
3 tbsp Butter

For the pudding: Mix and beat together sugar and eggs. Add dry ingredients alternately with the fruit juice. Pour into a greased Pyrex dish, bake at 350°F for 35 minutes.

Ten minutes before the pudding comes out of the oven, boil the sauce ingredients in a pot.

Bring to the boil for 5 minutes, stirring well. Prick the pudding and pour the sauce over the baked pudding.

Chocolate fudge

Leah Levine

Preparation time: 15mins

1/2 lb Sugar
1 cup Condensed Milk
1 cup Water
2 oz Chocolate
1 tsp Vanilla essence

Grease a saucepan before melting the sugar. Grate the chocolate and add to the sugar, with milk and water.

Place over a gentle heat and do not stir. When ready, fudge should form into a soft ball on testing in cold water. Add a small teaspoon of vanilla essence at this stage.

Cool, and beat until it hardens. Put into a greased tin and cut into squares.

Rachel's toffee

Rachel Levine

Preparation time: 35mins

2 lbs Sugar
1 tin Condensed Milk
The same quantity of water as milk
4 oz Butter
A few drops of Vanilla

Put the butter in the pan, then add sugar, milk and cold water.

Stir all until it boils and boil for 30 minutes stirring all the time until thick.

Add vanilla and pour into a buttered tin.

Memory

Leah and Rachel Levine were the sisters of Reverend Ephraim Levine – minister of the New West End Synagogue from 1916 to 1954.

Desserts

Chocolate mousse

Edwina Brown

Preparation time: 25mins
Cooling time required

~~~~~~~~~~~~~~~~~~~~

160g Dark Chocolate
(70% minimum)
10 Egg Whites
20g Sugar

Chop the chocolate finely and place into a bowl. Melt it over a pan of very hot water. Keep the heat very low. If the heat is too high the chocolate will granulate.

Whip the egg whites and sugar to soft peaks. Immediately, whisk in a quarter of the egg whites into the melted chocolate to lighten the base mixture. Then fold in the remaining egg whites with a spatula, ensuring that you do not over-mix as this would make the mousse heavy.

Pour into a glass bowl or individual glasses and allow to set in the fridge until required.

~~~~~~~~~~~~~~~~~~~~

Perfect pear tart tatin

Hassan Dervish, chef to Steven Wolfisz

Pre-heat your oven to 220°C
Preparation time: 15mins
Cooking time: 20mins

1 tin of Pears
4 oz Sugar
9 oz parev Puff Pastry

Drain the fruit, reserving the syrup. Reduce the syrup in a saucepan until very thick, taking care that it does not burn.

Meanwhile, prepare a caramel by dissolving the sugar in a little water in a wide, non-stick frying pan. Heat without stirring until the sugar becomes golden-brown. Reduce the heat and add the thick syrup very slowly. (Be careful not to burn yourself.)

Pour this caramel to cover the base of a greased 9 inch tart dish. Arrange the drained fruit on top in an attractive circular pattern.

Roll out the pastry on a little flour, to the shape of the dish (but slightly larger). Place the pastry over the fruit and tuck in the edges to seal. Bake in a hot oven (220°C) for about 15-20 minutes until the pastry is well risen and thoroughly cooked.

Remove the tart from the oven and cool for 5 minutes in the tin. Then carefully invert the tart onto a plate so that the fruit is now on top. Serve immediately (if possible) so that the pastry remains crisp.

Dairy noodle kugel

Shana Ballon

Pre-heat your oven to 350°F
Preparation time: 10mins
Cooking time: 1hour

Kugel:
16 oz Cottage Cheese
1 cup Soured Cream
5 Eggs
1/2 cup melted Margarine
or Butter
1 cup Sugar
2 tps Salt
1 lb Noodles,
cooked and drained
1/2 tsp Cinnamon and Allspice
or Nutmeg each, if desired
Dark or Golden Raisins if desired
(add according to taste)

Topping:
Crushed Cornflakes
1/4-1/3 cup ground Walnuts
or Pecans if desired
Sugar
Cinnamon

Combine all kugel ingredients. Pour into greased 9x13-inch baking pan.

Combine topping ingredients. Sprinkle kugel with topping. Bake at 350°F for 1 hour.

Best wishes and much love to our dear Rebbetzin, Anne Shisler, and to the entire Ladies Guild for their dedication and outstanding contributions to the NWES community. Eli and Shana Ballon

Stuffed peaches

Marcia Goodman

Pre-heat your oven to 180°C
Preparation time: 15mins
Cooking time: 30mins

5 Peaches
3 Macaroons,
better if they're slightly stale
1 oz zest of Lemon
4 oz castor Sugar
1/8 pint fresh Orange juice
(even better if you have some
white wine)

Cut the peaches in half and remove the stones.

Crumble the macaroons and put into a food processor or blender with the lemon zest and 1 oz of the sugar and 1 of the peaches.

Process until smooth. Spoon the stuffing into the halved peaches. Lay them in a buttered baking dish, pour over the orange juice (or white wine) and sprinkle with the remaining sugar.

Bake for 30 minutes at 180°C. Cool slightly before serving. Can be served at room temperature or warm.

Bon appetit!
from Marcia &
Perry Goodman

Bread & Cakes

Try our mouth watering selection of cakes, whether for a tea party, a seudah or even for Passover. If you're feeling adventurous, turn to the bread pages and impress your Shabbat guests with homemade challah.

⑦ Coffee gateau

Rosalind Coten, Rebbetzin, Ruislip Synagogue

Preparation time: 25mins

Gateau
1 lb Sponge Fingers
(Boudoir Biscuits)
1 pint strong Black Coffee

Sauce
6 oz Margarine
4 oz Sugar
2 Egg yolks
22 fl oz strong Black Coffee

Grease a 9 inch loose-bottomed tin. Dip the fingers in the coffee quickly and layer the bottom of the tin. Stand undipped fingers like soldiers around the side.

Melt the margarine, combine all the sauce ingredients and leave to cool. Pour a layer of sauce over the sponge fingers. Add another layer of dipped sponge fingers. Cover with a layer of sauce. Decorate with cream and walnuts.

Chocolate crispy cake

Tina Son

Preparation time: 20mins

8 oz good quality
Cooking Chocolate
1/2 Block Margarine
Rice Krispies
Handful Mini Marshmallows

Melt margarine in a large bowl in the microwave. Add chocolate broken into small pieces and half of the marshmallows and melt in microwave for around 2 minutes 30 seconds on high in 650 microwave, or medium in 850 microwave. Stir well until smooth and then add Rice Krispies until all of the chocolate mix is used up.

Break marshmallows in half, reserve a few and add rest to the Rice Krispie mix, stir well. Spread the mix on a large plate or platter and smooth out. Decorate with remaining marshmallows.

Put in the fridge to harden. Eat and enjoy!

Tip

A true favourite for kids - get them decorating!

Superb spiced banana cake

Shana Ballon

Pre-heat your oven to 175°C
Preparation time: 20mins
Cooking time: 30mins

1/2 cup Butter or Margarine, softened
1 cup packed Light Brown Sugar
1/2 cup Caster sugar
1$\frac{1}{4}$ tsp ground Allspice
1/2 tsp ground Nutmeg
2 Eggs
1$\frac{1}{2}$ tsp Vanilla extract
1$\frac{1}{4}$ cups All-purpose Flour
3/4 cup Rolled Oats
1/2 tsp Baking soda
3/4 tsp Baking Powder
1/4 tsp Salt
1/3 cup Sour Cream
1 cup mashed Bananas

Grease and lightly flour two 9 inch round (or square) cake pans.

Combine flour, oats, baking soda, baking powder and salt in a medium sized bowl. In a large bowl, cream the butter or margarine. Add sugars and spices; beat until light and fluffy. Mix in eggs and vanilla extract. Add 1/3 of the dry ingredients to the butter mixture; mix well. Add the sour cream; mix well. Add another 1/3 of the dry ingredients; mix well. Add half the bananas; mix well. Repeat with remaining dry ingredients and bananas. Pour batter into prepared pans.

Bake until cake is done, about 30 minutes. After cooling, frost with icing of your choice, or none at all.

Chef's note

Makes a lovely layer cake with a wide assortment of possible fillings or icings. Also tastes divine topped with vanilla custard and fresh fruit.

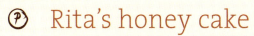

Rita's honey cake

Sandra Blackman

Pre-heat your oven to 180°C
Preparation time: 10mins
Cooking time: 1hour

8 oz Self-raising flour
1¹ᐟ² tsp Bicarbonate of soda
1¹ᐟ² tsp Cinnamon
1¹ᐟ² tsp mixed Spice
1¹ᐟ² tsp ground Ginger
1 cup Oil
1 cup hot Water
1 cup Sugar
1 lb tin Golden Syrup
3 Eggs

Mix all ingredients together. Put into a deep baking tin as it rises really high. Do not use spring-form or loose-bottom pan as it will leak.

Bake at 180°C for 1 hour.

⑫ Apple torte

Angela Taylor

Pre-heat your oven to 180°C
Preparation time: 20mins
Cooking time: 40-55mins

Cake
3 Eggs
7 oz Caster Sugar
20g pack Vanilla Sugar
6 fl oz Oil
3 oz Potato Flour
3 oz Cakemeal
1½ tsp Baking Powder
Granulated sugar
for sprinkling

Filling
3 large Baking Apples
3 tbsp Granulated Sugar mixed
with 1 tsp Cinnamon

Grease a square 9 inch tin.

Peel, core and grate the apples coarsely. Add cinnamon and sugar. Mix well.

Whisk eggs and sugars till thick and lemon coloured. Whisk in oil, followed by dry ingredients. Pour half the sponge mixture into the tin. Smooth it level. Spoon the apple mixture on top. Cover with the remainder of the sponge mixture. Sprinkle the top with granulated sugar.

Bake for 40-55 minutes at 180°C until well risen and firm to gentle touch in centre.

Hot baked cheesecake

The Jewish Princess

Pre-heat your oven to 200°C
Preparation time: 15mins
Cooking time: 50mins

Olive Oil, for greasing
1.2kg full-fat Cream Cheese
(eg Philadelphia)
400g Caster Sugar
3 large Eggs
200ml Double Cream
100g Cornflour
30g Instant Vanilla pudding
(Osem)
1 teaspoon Vanilla essence
Icing sugar, for dusting

Grease a 30cm x 20cm ovenproof dish with olive oil.

In a large mixing bowl, beat together the cheese, caster sugar and 2 eggs. Add the cream, cornflour, instant vanilla pudding, vanilla essence and the other egg. Beat until smooth. Pour the ingredients into the prepared ovenproof dish.

Place a large baking tray filled with water in the oven. Put the ovenproof dish on the baking tray; the water should come three-quarters of the way up the side of the cheesecake. Bake the cake for approximately 20 minutes, or until the top is a light golden colour.

Turn the temperature down to 160°C/325°F/gas mark 3 for approximately 30 minutes, or until set. Serve warm.

From The Jewish Princess
Guide to Fabulosity,
printed by Quadrille.
www.thejewishprincess.com

Chef's note

This typical hot baked cheesecake is traditionally served at breakfast, but my motto of anytime, anyplace, anywhere applies here.

Miniature (iced) Chanukah cakes

Alan Gainsford

Pre-heat your oven to 180°C
Makes 30

550g ground Almonds
450g Caster Sugar
5 Eggs
Peel of a Lemon
2 tbsp Flour
100g Mixed Peel
2 tsp Mixed Spice
Cinnamon to taste
A little Cocoa for colour

Beat eggs and sugar until creamy. Add all the other ingredients slowly. The mixture should be stiff.

Form small round cakes and place on baking tray with rice paper. Bake well at 180°C.

Next day ice them with white or pink icing. When dry keep them in a tin.

Almond pudding

Anne Shisler

Pre-heat your oven to 170°C
Preparation time: 15mins
Cooking time: 45mins

4 oz ground Almonds
4 Eggs
3 oz Caster Sugar

Separate eggs and beat whites until stiff. Whip yolks and sugar until light and fluffy, add the ground almonds and beaten egg whites and beat for another 3 or 4 minutes. Turn into a greased baking dish and bake at 170°C for about 45-50 minutes. Serve hot or cold, sprinkled with caster sugar.

Note

Passover recipe!

Polish cake

Sylvia Sherwood

8 oz crushed Digestive Biscuits
4 oz Margarine
1 dessert spoon Cocoa
1 tbsp Golden Syrup
6 oz Chocolate

Mix all ingredients except the chocolate and press into a 7 inch square tin. Melt chocolate and pour over the top. Refrigerate for 1 hour.

Tip

An easy-to-make fridge cake – no baking required!

Apple cake

Patricia Fisher

Pre-heat your oven to 180°C
Cooking time: 1hour

7 oz Self-raising Flour
5 oz soft Margarine
3 oz Caster Sugar
1 large Egg
1 lb cooking Apples
1 tbsp Granulated Sugar
Squeeze of Lemon juice
2 tbsp Apricot jam

Put flour, margarine, caster sugar and egg in a bowl and beat to a smooth batter. If it seems a bit too thick, add a dash of hot water. Spread two thirds of the mixture into a well greased 8 inch loose-bottom cake tin.

Peel core and slice the apples thinly. Place slices over the batter, sprinkle with granulated sugar and lemon juice, and dot the jam over it. Then dot the remainder of the batter over the top. Bake for an hour at 180°C. Nicer served hot and you can dredge it with icing sugar.

Chef's note

If I don't have apricot jam I use marmalade. Raisins or berries can be added if desired.

Best wishes from
Patricia, David, Joseph
and Simon Fisher

Ina Garten lemon yogurt cake

Brian Ward, Head of English, City of London School for Girls

Pre-heat your oven to 350°F
Preparation time: 15mins
Cooking time: 50mins

Cake
1/2 cups All-purpose Flour
2 tsp Baking Powder
1/2 tsp Salt
1 cup plain Whole-milk Yogurt
$1^{1/3}$ cups Sugar, divided
3 extra-large Eggs
2 tsp grated Lemon zest
(2 lemons)
1/2 tsp pure Vanilla extract
1/2 cup Vegetable Oil
1/3 cup freshly squeezed
Lemon juice

Glaze
1 cup Icing Sugar
2 tbsp freshly squeezed
Lemon juice

Grease an $8^{1/2}$ x $4^{1/4}$ x $2^{1/2}$ inch loaf pan. Line the bottom with parchment paper. Grease and flour the pan.

Sift together the flour, baking powder, and salt into a bowl. In another bowl, whisk together the yogurt, 1 cup sugar, eggs, lemon zest, and vanilla. Slowly whisk the dry ingredients into the wet ingredients. With a rubber spatula, fold the vegetable oil into the batter, making sure it's all incorporated. Pour the batter into the prepared pan and bake for about 50 minutes, or until a cake tester placed in the centre of the loaf comes out clean. Meanwhile, cook the 1/3 cup lemon juice and remaining 1/3 cup sugar in a small pan until the sugar dissolves and the mixture is clear. Set aside.

When the cake is done, allow it to cool in the pan for 10 minutes. Carefully place on a baking rack over a sheet pan. While the cake is still warm, pour the lemon-sugar mixture over the cake and allow it to soak in. Cool.

For the glaze, combine the icing sugar and lemon juice and pour over the cake.

ⓓ Sour cream cake

Jean Ha, Music Department, City of London School for Girls

Pre-heat your oven to 350°F
Preparation time: 25mins
Cooking time: 45mins

2 cups Pastry Flour
1 tsp Baking Powder
1/4 tsp Salt
1/2 lb Unsalted Butter
at room temp
3/4 cup White Sugar
2 Eggs, room temp
1 tsp Vanilla extract
1 cup Sour cream, room temp
1 tsp Baking Soda
Cinnamon sugar
(4 or 5 parts sugar to 1 part
cinnamon – to taste)
Chopped walnuts for
sprinkling (optional)

Grease a 9 inch spring form/round cake tin or 14 inch loaf pan.

Sift flour and measure. Add baking powder and salt, and sift three times. Set aside. In a separate bowl, cream butter and sugar. Set aside. Beat eggs and then add vanilla. Pour the egg mixture into the creamed butter and whisk well.

Add baking soda to sour cream and gently stir just until mixed. The sour cream should get foamy. This should be done just before you're ready to make the batter.

Add flour and sour cream alternately to the creamed butter mixture. I do it in about 4 portions (start with flour, then add a bit of sour cream, flour again, then sour cream, etc). Make sure all the flour is mixed well into the butter mixture before adding sour cream. Use a spatula and take care not to over-mix.

Pour batter into the pan, sprinkle with the cinnamon sugar and walnuts, and bake for 45 minutes. Let it cool in the pan for 5 minutes, then completely on a wire rack.

Plava Cake

Priscilla Graham

Pre-heat your oven to 180°C
Preparation time: 15mins.
Cooking time: 45mins

6 large Eggs
2 cups Caster Sugar
1 heaped tbsp Potato Flour
1 cup fine Matzo Meal
3 tbsp boiling Water

Beat yolks and sugar until pale. Whip whites until stiff (with a pinch of salt). Sieve the potato flour and matzo meal together. Add alternate spoonfuls of whites and the flour/meal mixture to the yolk mixture. Add the boiling water.

Bake in a 10 inch square tin lined with greaseproof paper at 180°C for 45 minutes. Cool and turn out.

Note

Passover recipe!

With best wishes
from Cantor
Jeremy Lawson

Carrot and almond cake

Silvia Nacamulli

Pre-heat your oven to 180°C
Preparation time: 20mins
Cooking time: 40mins

200g finely crushed Carrots
200g finely crushed Almonds
200g White Caster Sugar
4 free range Eggs
A pinch of Salt
A handful of Breadcrumbs
or Matzo Meal
Margarine for greasing
Icing sugar to decorate

Separate the egg whites from the yolks. Beat the egg yolks with the sugar until you have a creamy consistency. Add the finely crushed almonds and carrots and mix thoroughly.

In a separate bowl beat the egg whites until they become very stiff. Slowly add the egg whites to the rest of the mixture. Add a pinch of salt and mix well but gently. Take a 24cm (9 inch) diameter round spring form baking tray and spread a thin layer of margarine all around the inside of it. Spread the breadcrumbs/matzo meal on the margarine so as to create a thin coat (it will stick around the sides) and discard the extra. Pour the mixture into the tray and leave to bake for 40 minutes. To check if the cake is cooked insert a skewer or toothpick; if the cake is cooked it will come out dry and clean.

Wait at least half an hour before removing the cake from the baking tray, and then place on a large plate. With a small sieve spread some icing sugar on top to decorate. You can serve the dessert on its own or with some cream and fresh berries on the side.

Tip

If you have a food processor use it to mix the ingredients together as this will crush and blend them

Silvia Nacamulli is a freelance cook, teacher and writer of Italian cooking. Her specialty is Italian Jewish cooking and today she is an authority in the subject. Born and bred in Rome, Silvia came to London in 1998. She has run her own business since 2002, 'La Cucina di Silvia – Cooking for the soul'. She has a regular cookery column in the Jewish Chronicle and has taught at the Divertimenti cookery school for several years.

www.cookingforthesoul.com

cooking for the soul...

Carrot cake

Abi Warren

Pre-heat your oven to 180°C
Preparation time: 25mins
Cooking time: 25mins

Cake
250ml Vegetable Oil
4 Eggs, beaten
225g soft Light Brown Sugar
140g Carrots, peeled and grated
225g Self-raising Flour
1/2 tsp Bicarbonate of Soda
2 tsp Ground Cinnamon
1 tsp Ground Ginger
140g chopped Walnuts

Icing
45g Unsalted Butter
170g Cream Cheese (full fat!)
300g Icing Sugar
1 tsp Vanilla extract

Stir together the oil, eggs, sugar and carrots. Sift into a bowl the flour, bicarbonate, cinnamon and ginger. Fold together then fold in the walnuts.

Divide mixture between 2 tins and bake for 25 minutes. Leave to cool in the tins for 10 minutes then turn out and cool completely.

To make the icing beat the butter and cream cheese together, add icing sugar and beat until smooth. Flavour with vanilla extract. Use icing to sandwich cakes together and ice the top. Decorate with walnuts or sugar carrots.

With best wishes from
Abi and Ben Warren.
abi@cakesbakesandsparkles.co.uk

Easy fruit cake

Annette Weinberg

Pre-heat your oven to 140°C
Preparation time: 15mins
Cooking time: 1hour 40mins

6 oz soft brown Sugar
4 oz soft Margarine
Small tin crushed Pineapple,
drained
8 oz Self-raising Flour
2 Eggs
12 oz Mixed Fruit
4 oz chopped Glacé Cherries

Put all ingredients, except flour and eggs, into a large saucepan on a low light and allow to melt slowly. Stir until the mixture boils. Take off the heat and cool and then add flour and eggs. Mix well.

Grease an 8 inch round tin and pour in the mixture. Decorate the top with almonds. Bake for 1 hour and 40 minutes at 140°C

Chef's note { Great for a Shabbat Seudah.

Cottage cheese doughnuts

Felicity Miller

Preparation time: 25mins
Makes 15 doughnuts

2$^{1/2}$ cups Plain Flour (sifted)
2 x 453g containers Low Fat Cottage Cheese
4 Eggs
1/3 cup Vegetable Oil
1/2 tsp Baking Powder
1/4 tsp Cinnamon
2 tsp Lemon rind
1/4 tsp Salt
1/2 cup Caster Sugar
Icing Sugar for decoration

In a bowl mix the flour, cottage cheese, eggs, oil, baking powder, lemon rind, cinnamon, salt and sugar. Mix well.

Heat oil in a pan until very hot. Make little round balls from the dough (about 2.5cms in diameter). Roll the little balls in flour and fry until light brown.

Drain on a paper towel. Sprinkle with powdered sugar.

Tip
Best served hot!

Banana cake

Bella Shapiro

Pre-heat your oven to 190°C
Preparation time: 15mins
Cooking time: 45mins

2¼ cups fine Plain Flour
2 tsp Baking Powder
1/4 tsp Bicarbonate of Soda
1¼ cups granulated Brown Sugar
1/2 cup Margarine
1 cup well-mashed Bananas
2 tsp Lemon juice
1/2 cup plus 1 tbsp Alpro Soya Cream
1/2 tsp Vanilla essence
2 Eggs

Beat margarine, bananas and vanilla essence at high speed for 2 minutes, then add 2 eggs.

Sift flour, baking powder, bicarbonate of soda and sugar into a bowl.

Gradually beat half the dry ingredients into the banana mixture and add lemon juice. Add the remaining dry ingredients together with the Alpro soya cream.

Pour into a greased and floured oblong cake pan. Bake at 190°C for 45 minutes until golden brown. Remove from pan when cool.

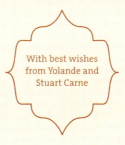

With best wishes
from Yolande and
Stuart Carne

Apple sponge pudding

Anne Shisler

Pre-heat your oven to 180°C
Preparation time: 15mins
Cooking time: 45mins

4 Apples, peeled and sliced
10 oz Sugar
1 tbsp Raisins
1 tbsp chopped
blanched almonds
1 tbsp White wine
4 Eggs separated
Grated rind of 1 Lemon
1/2 cup fine Matzo Meal
Pinch of salt
Cinnamon to taste

Mix sliced apples with raisins, cinnamon, almonds and wine and 1 tablespoon of sugar. Add a little water and cook gently for a few minutes so apples begin to soften (on hob or in microwave).

Beat egg yolks and remaining sugar until light and fluffy. Blend in lemon rind and matzo meal. Beat egg whites with salt until stiff and fold into batter. Bake at 180°C for 45 minutes.

Note

Passover recipe!

Cheese and onion bread

Erica Wyld

Pre-heat your oven to Gas mark 5
Preparation time: 25mins
Cooking time: 40mins

Dough
8 fl oz hot Water
1 lb strong Bread Flour
1 sachet Yeast
1 tbsp Sugar
2 tsp Salt
2 tbsp Oil
1 Egg

Filling
2 oz Unsalted Butter
1$^{1/2}$ tbsp Oil
1 bunch Spring Onions
and stalks
3 tbsp Parmesan Cheese
5 tbsp Poppy Seeds

Glaze
1 Egg yolk + 2 tsp Water
4 tbsp Poppy Seeds

Mix the yeast with the other dry ingredients, then add all the other dough ingredients and knead thoroughly. Cover and leave in the fridge till double the size (9-12 hours).

Chop the onions. Sauté them in the oil and butter, remove, and stir in the cheese and poppy seeds. Cool for 10 minutes. Roll the dough to approximately 12 inches long, cut into three 4 inch strips and spoon one third of the filling down each strip. Fold each strip to secure the filling. Place on a greased tray, plait the strips, place in a plastic carrier bag and leave to double its size – 45 minutes. Brush with the glaze, sprinkle with poppy seeds and bake, gas mark 5, for 40 minutes. Cool thoroughly.

Chef's note

I use both oil and butter for sautéing because butter tastes better but oil burns at a higher temperature so it is better for frying.

No-fuss rolls

Shana Ballon

Pre-heat your oven to 230°C
Preparation time: 10mins
Cooking time: 10mins

125g Self-raising Flour
120ml semi-skimmed Milk
or non-dairy equivalent
30ml Mayonnaise
2g Sugar

In a small bowl, combine all of the ingredients. Spoon into six muffin cups coated with non-stick cooking spray.

Bake at 230°C for 8-10 minutes or until a toothpick comes out clean.

Cool for 5 minutes before removing from pan to a wire rack.

Tip

Serve warm with butter, jam or your favourite spread.

Penina's challah

Shana Ballon

Pre-heat your oven to 180°C
Preparation time: 3hours
Cooking time: 45mins
Makes 2 large loaves

500ml lukewarm Water
1¹ᐟ²-2 tbsp active dry Yeast
1 Egg, beaten
3/4 cup Oil
1kg strong White Bread Flour
1/2 cup Granulated White Sugar
2 tsp Salt
Egg for glazing

Dissolve yeast into water. Stir in sugar and salt and then mix in the beaten egg. Combine well. Add oil, mix again until frothy. Lastly, pour the liquids into the flour.

Knead until well combined and elastic. The dough will be a bit sticky but will still hold its shape. Allow it to rise in lightly oiled bowl covered with cling film or a large damp towel for 2-3 hours or until doubled in bulk.

Shape loaves as desired. Place on baking trays covered with parchment paper.

Bake large loaves for 35-45 minutes or until bottom sounds hollow when tapped. In a fan oven, this should be closer to 45 minutes. For rolls or smaller loaves, approximately 25-35 minutes – use your judgment.

Bread & Cakes

Biscuits

Alan Gainsford suggests the following 'simple solution' biscuit recipe:
"Purchase return bus ticket to Golders Green. Proceed to Carmelli's and order 2 lbs of 'kichels'. Return to either home or New West End shul and consume with pot of tea!" Alternatively you could try some of these…

Wonderful brownies

Priscilla Graham

Pre-heat your oven to 400°F
Preparation time: 15mins
Cooking time: 30mins

1 cup Unsalted Butter
8 oz unsweetened Chocolate
5 large Eggs
3$^{1/2}$cups Sugar
2 tsp Instant Coffee
1 tbsp Vanilla
1$^{1/3}$ cups Plain Flour
1/2 cup Chocolate Chips
1 cup chopped roast Walnuts

Grease a 9 inch x 13 inch pan.
Melt chocolate and butter (in a double boiler, if possible).

Beat eggs, sugar and coffee for 10 minutes, reduce speed and add melted chocolate. Slowly add flour and mix. Fold in chocolate chips and nuts.

Bake until edges are dry and centre is soft, approximately 30 minutes.

Tip

Using the best quality chocolate available is the secret of the deep, rich chocolate flavour.

Gingerbread biscuits

Sharlott Toube

Pre-heat your oven to 180°C
Preparation time: 40mins
Cooking time: 5mins

2 oz Caster Sugar
4 oz Golden Syrup
4 oz Treacle
3 tbsp parev Margarine
1 tbsp Water
8 oz Plain Flour
1/2 tsp Bicarbonate of Soda
1/4 tsp Baking Powder
1 tsp Ginger
1 tsp freshly ground Cinnamon
1/4 tsp freshly ground Allspice
1/4 tsp freshly ground Clove
1/4 tsp freshly ground Nutmeg

Combine caster sugar, golden syrup, treacle, margarine and water in a saucepan and bring to the boil, stirring, before removing the pan from the heat to cool.

Sift flour, bicarbonate of soda, baking powder, ginger and spices together. Combine the liquid and dry ingredients and knead for at least 5 minutes to a firmish, pliable dough, adding a little more water if required. Rest in the refrigerator for 30 minutes or more before rolling in batches (1/8 inch / 3mm thick) between sheets of cling-film. Cut out suitable shapes.

Bake on baking parchment at 180°C (160°C in a fan oven) for 5 minutes or more, until just firm. (They do stiffen up while cooling.) Remove with care and place on racks. When completely cool, store in an airtight tin.

Chef's note

Admittedly, cut-out biscuits are rather time-consuming to bake, but they are definitely worth the effort. After all, if you are a grandmother, such clauses are written into your contract, so GO FOR IT

Almond Florentines

Gaby Morris

Pre-heat your oven to 150°C
Preparation time: 20mins
Cooking time: 12mins

2 Free-range Egg whites
100g Icing Sugar
260g flaked Almonds
Grated zest of 1 Orange
Small amount of Vegetable Oil

Chef's note

Great after meat or dairy meals and for Passover too. For a richer version paint one side with melted dark chocolate.

Line a heavy baking tray with parchment paper brushed with a little vegetable oil.

Put the egg whites, sugar, flaked almond and the grated zest of an orange in a bowl. Mix together gently to bind the mixture.

By your side prepare a small bowl of cold water. Dip your hand in the bowl of water and pick up a portion of the mixture and put it in a small mound on the lined baking tray. Leave enough space between the portions for the mixture to spread. Using a folk gently flatten the mixture as much as you can without creating gaps between the almonds. Each Florentine should be 6-8cm.

Bake for 12 minutes or until the biscuits are golden coloured. After cooling for 5 minutes, remove the biscuits from the parchment paper they were baked on, to a fresh piece of parchment paper – it helps them to stay in one piece.

" "
*With best wishes from
Gaby, Howard,
Josh and Lucy*
" "

George & Joseph's
o' so simple oat biscuits

Toni Nagel

Pre-heat your oven to 160°C
Preparation time: 20mins
Cooking time: 10mins

75g Plain Flour
75g Porridge Oats
1/2 tsp Bicarbonate of Soda
60g Sugar
75g Margarine
1 tbsp Golden Syrup

Melt the margarine and golden syrup together. Put all the other ingredients into a bowl. Pour the melted ingredients into the dry ones and mix together.

Roll into small balls and flatten with a fork onto greaseproof paper. Bake at 160°C for 10 minutes.

When done, biscuits should look golden. Don't worry if they are a bit soft when recommended cooking time is up – as long as they are the right colour, they'll be perfect once cooled!

> *Enjoy – Martin and*
> *Jennifer Melman*

Auntie Nancy's biscuits

Caryl Harris

Pre-heat your oven to 190°C
Preparation time: 20mins

6 oz Self-raising Flour
4 oz Butter or soft Margarine
2 oz Caster Sugar

Put butter into flour, add sugar (it may need a little cold water). Mix to a very smooth dough, until all cracks are out. Roll out thinly, cut into rounds, put on a greased biscuit tray, not too close together.

Bake at 190°C or gas mark 5 until light brown. Place near top of oven if not fan assisted.

> 66
> *Memory:*
> *I remember coming home from nursery and opening the back door to the gorgeous smell of wet sheets drying on a clothes horse in front of the fire and my Aunt Nancy taking these biscuits out of the oven – almost my very first memory.*
> 99

Chocolate chip cookies

Shana Ballon

Pre-heat your oven to 180°C
Preparation time: 20mins
Cooking time: 12mins
Makes: 45 cookies

2 cups Sugar
2 Eggs
1 cup Oil
2 packets Vanilla Sugar
(approx. 2 tbsp)
3¼ cups very finely ground
Almonds (almost flour
consistency – if necessary,
blend or process to finer grain)
1 cup Potato Flour
1¼ cups Chocolate Chips

Cream together the sugar, eggs and oil. Add in the vanilla, almonds, potato flour and chocolate chips and mix well. Freeze the batter for 10 minutes to make it easier to form the cookies.

Make small balls out of the batter using your hands. Place them on a parchment paper lined tray. DO NOT flatten the cookies!

Bake them for 12 minutes until they are lightly browned and crinkled. Let them cool a bit on the paper and then remove to a wire rack to cool completely. These freeze very well.

Note

Passover recipe!

Biscuits

The best ginger biscuits

Anne Shisler

Pre-heat your oven to 190°C
Preparation time: 20mins
Cooking time: 15mins

350g Plain Flour
100g Margarine
175g soft Brown Sugar
4 level tbsp Golden Syrup
1 level tbsp ground Ginger
1 level tsp Bicarbonate Soda
1 Egg

Sieve the flour, ginger and soda. Rub in the margarine. Add sugar, stir in syrup and egg. Knead on a floured board. Roll out and cut into shapes. Prick with a fork.

Bake on greased baking trays at 190°C/gas mark 5 for 10-15 minutes depending on your oven – a fan oven will be a bit faster.

Over the years I have collected a wonderful collection of different shaped biscuit cutters, including of course a gingerbread man.

Tip

Get your children or grandchildren to help you with these.

66

Happy eating from the Shisler grandchildren: Alfie and Sadie Warren, with Evie and Felix Shisler

99

Chocolate logs

Hilary Myers

Preparation time: 30 mins

4 oz Margarine
8 oz Icing Sugar
6 oz Coconut
2 oz chopped Nuts
1 tsp Instant Coffee
Chocolate to cover

Dissolve coffee in a small quantity of water.

Cream the margarine and sugar, then add coconut, chopped nuts and coffee. Form into fingers. Place in the fridge to go firm.

Melt chocolate in double boiler or microwave and submerge the fingers in it one at a time, removing them carefully with a fork or spatula. Place on baking paper to harden. Pack in tiny paper cases and place in a plastic box in the fridge or freezer.

" This recipe was given to me by my stepmother, Sophie Levy (neé Sprince) of Liverpool. "

My mother's biscuits

Natalie Cutler

Pre-heat your oven to 350°F
Preparation time: 15mins

8 oz Margarine
3/4 breakfast cup Sugar
1 Egg
3-4 cups Self-raising Flour
Flavouring of choice (optional)

Cream sugar and margarine. Add beaten egg. Slowly stir in flour until pliable and not too sticky. Make into small balls. Flatten slightly and mark with a fork.

Put onto an ungreased tin and bake at 350°F until slightly brown.

Congratulations to everyone involved in this 'delicious' project, Natalie and Michael Cutler

Oatmeal, cherry and walnut biscuits

Felicity Miller

Pre-heat your oven to 175°C
Preparation time: 20mins
Cooking time: 12-13mins

150g White Sugar
165g packed Brown Sugar
160g Butter or Margarine
2 Eggs
30ml Milk or Water
5g Baking Soda
5g Baking Powder
6g Salt
2g ground Cinnamon
5ml Vanilla extract
125g All-purpose Flour
245g Quick cooking oats
115g chopped Walnuts
160g dried Cherries

In a mixer bowl, combine the white sugar, brown sugar and butter/margarine. Beat until smooth and creamy. Add the eggs one at a time mixing well after each one. Beat the mixture until well combined.

Mix in the milk/water, baking soda, baking powder, salt, cinnamon and vanilla to the egg mixture. Beat for one minute. Add the flour and mix until incorporated. Add the walnuts and mix again. Add the oats one cup at a time, mixing well after each addition. Stir in the dried cherries and mix just until they are distributed evenly.

Drop heaping tablespoonfuls of batter about 2 inches apart on ungreased cookie sheets. Do not shape them; they will spread evenly during the baking process. Bake at 175°C for 12-13 minutes. The tops of the biscuits should just turn a light golden brown. Remove the biscuits from the oven and let sit on the sheets for about 5 minutes before moving the biscuits to cooling racks. Let biscuits cool to room temperature then place in airtight containers for storage.

Peanut butter and fudge brownies
with salted peanuts

Chaya Mansdorf

Pre-heat your oven to 325°F
Preparation time: 45mins
Cooking time: 30mins
Makes: 30 brownies

Tip

Ganache is a French term for a mixture of chocolate and cream.

Brownies
3/4 cup Unsalted butter
7 oz bittersweet Chocolate
3 oz unsweetened Chocolate
1¹ᐟ² cups Sugar
1¹ᐟ² tsp Vanilla extract
1/4 tsp Salt
4 large Eggs
1 cup All-purpose Flour
1 cup roasted Salted Peanuts

Frosting and ganache
1 cup crunchy Peanut butter
1/2 cup Unsalted butter
3/4 cup powdered Icing Sugar
1/8 tsp Salt
1/8 tsp ground Nutmeg
1 tbsp whole Milk
1 tsp Vanilla extract
7 oz bittersweet Chocolate

Position rack in centre of oven and preheat to 325°F. Line 13 x 9 x 2 inch baking tray with foil, leaving long overhang; grease the foil.

For the brownies: Chop both chocolates and roughly chop the peanuts. Place 3/4 cup butter in heavy large saucepan. Add the chocolates; stir over low heat until smooth. Remove from heat. Whisk in sugar, vanilla and salt, then eggs, one at a time. Fold in flour, then nuts. Spread in the prepared baking tray. Bake until tester inserted into centre comes out with moist crumbs attached – about 30 minutes. Place tray on a rack to cool.

For the frosting and ganache: Divide the butter in half. Using an electric mixer, beat the peanut butter and 1/4 cup butter in a medium bowl to blend. Beat in icing sugar, salt and nutmeg, then milk and vanilla. Spread the frosting over brownies.

Stir chocolate and 1/4 cup butter in heavy small saucepan over low heat until smooth. Drop the ganache all over the frosting; spread to cover. Chill until set, about 1¹ᐟ² hours. Cover and keep chilled. Transfer brownie cake to work surface; cut into squares. Bring to room temperature; serve.

Fee's pistachio ribbon bars

Shana Ballon

Pre-heat your oven to 160°C
Preparation time: 15mins
Cooking time: 45mins

8 oz Unsalted Margarine, softened
1 cup Granulated sugar
1 large Egg
2 cups All-purpose Flour
1/8 tsp Salt (omit this if your pistachios are salted!)
1/2 - 2/3 cup Raspberry or Strawberry jam
2/3 cup Pistachios, chopped

Combine margarine, sugar and egg. Beat until thoroughly blended. Stir in flour and salt. Spread half the dough into a 23cm square pan. Bake for 10 minutes, then remove from the oven.

Spread jam to within half an inch of the edge of the dough.

Add pistachios to the remaining dough and combine. Drop spoonfuls of the mixture over the jam to cover it.

Bake for 35 minutes longer, until the top is golden brown. Remove from the oven and cool in the pan.

Cut into squares. Store in an air-tight container.

Chef's note

This recipe was shared by my friend Fiona and is a family holiday favourite in her German hometown.

Index

MESSAGES FROM
OUR PLATINUM SPONSORS

*Happy Eating from all the
Millers: Frank, Felicity, Alex,
Ben and Josh*

*Family Gainsford are
delighted to support
the New West End Guild*

*With best wishes from
the Rosenfeld family*

MESSAGES FROM OUR GOLD SPONSORS

Best wishes from Jacquie and Stuart Katz

Susan and Harvey Katz wish the New West End Guild every success

The Lando Family wishes the cookery book every success

MESSAGES FROM OUR SILVER SPONSORS

*For our wonderful Mother, Denise Lux,
whose love, nurturing and nourishment
has always been an inspiration.
From Danielle and Collette*

*The way to a man's heart is through his
stomach. Harry Sieratzki with mother
Barbara and Bencie*

*With love and best wishes always,
Angela, Jon, Rachel and Zac Skry*

*Denise and Melvyn Lux wish the Guild
every success with the New West End
Cookery Book*

*Hilary and David Slovick hungrily await
the outcome of this excellent project*

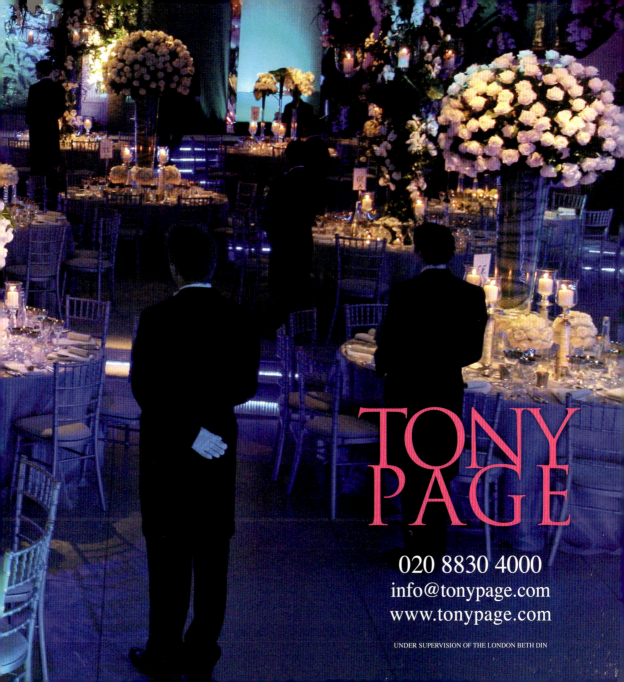

TONY
PAGE

020 8830 4000
info@tonypage.com
www.tonypage.com

UNDER SUPERVISION OF THE LONDON BETH DIN

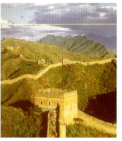

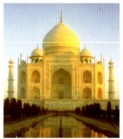

Pettitts

Imagine the journey of a lifetime...
...then let us arrange it for you

For over 20 years Pettitts' well-travelled team of specialists has been creating unique itineraries for clients who demand the very best professional service – over three-quarters of our business comes from repeat clients and recommendations.

Whether your interests are culture, wildlife watching, just relaxing in beautiful exotic surroundings or enjoying a city's hustle and bustle, the choice is yours.

Our aim is to meet your exact requirements. You decide how fast or slow you want the itinerary to be – what days you want to travel, what days at leisure. What you want to do and see, what type of accommodation you prefer – you make all the decisions, whilst we provide the friendly expert advice and inside knowledge to help you. We are always delighted to provide a full written quotation without any obligation.

**INDIA • NEPAL • BHUTAN • SRI LANKA • THAILAND • CAMBODIA
LAOS • VIETNAM • MALAYSIA • BORNEO • CHINA • JAPAN • MOROCCO
EGYPT • ARMENIA • TURKEY • ARGENTINA • CHILE • PERU • ECUADOR
BRAZIL • GALAPAGOS ISLANDS • ANTARCTICA**

Pettitts, Bayham House, 12-16 Grosvenor Road, Tunbridge Wells, Kent TN1 2AB
Tel: 01892 515966 • Fax: 01892 521500

www.pettitts.co.uk

Established 1988

EXCLUSIVE JOURNEYS FOR THE INDEPENDENT TRAVELLER

ABTA V5041   ATOL 2841

LOUIS MANN
& SON LTD

LICENSED KOSHER BUTCHER
Poulterer & Delicatessen

CATERED PARTIES
DAILY DELIVERIES

0208 958 5945/4910
email: Louismannltd@aol.com

Dear ALL Readers,

We hope you enjoy making, cooking and (eating) these recipes!

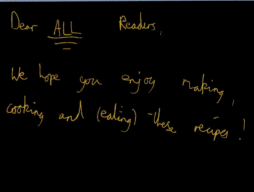

Joseph, Michael, Toni and George Rosenfeld

The New West End
Synagogue Guild

Generations

Over 100 recipes from
a culinary community

©2010 The New West End Synagogue

Published by Creative Interpartners, London
Email: ci@creativeinterpartners.co.uk

ISBN: 978-0-9566706-0-1